One Thought Scares Me...

We Teach Our Children
What We Wish Them to Know;
We Don't Teach Our Children
What We Don't Wish Them to Know

RICHARD DREYFUSS
ACADEMY AWARD WINNER

SKYHORSE PUBLISHING

Skyhorse Publishing books may be purchased in bulk at special discounts for sales promotion, corporate gifts, fund-raising, or educational purposes. Special editions can also be created to specifications. For details, contact the Special Sales Department, Skyhorse Publishing, 307 West 36th Street, 11th Floor, New York, NY 10018 or info@ skyhorsepublishing.com.

Skyhorse® and Skyhorse Publishing® are registered trademarks of Skyhorse Publishing, Inc.®, a Delaware corporation.

Visit our website at www.skyhorsepublishing.com.

10 9 8 7 6 5 4 3 2 1

Library of Congress Cataloging-in-Publication Data is available on file.

Cover design by Brian Peterson

Print ISBN: 978-1-5107-7612-8
Ebook ISBN: 978-1-5107-7613-5

Printed in the United States of America

To my wife Svetlana,
for showing me what love truly is.
The key is sharing.

Contents

I have some questions:

Why did we remove the subject of Civics from our public schools?

Why have we made it impossible to give our children even a glimpse of the reality of running our government before it's their turn to run the government?

When and why did we stop telling our children that we were responsible for a revolution in governance that was the first ever to free the minds of the entire human race and firmly commit to our belief in the potential of the poor?

Why have we kept all this completely unknowable by our progeny for the past fifty years?

Why have we refused to even discuss this stupid and self-destructive act?

Introduction

David Sarnoff was an immigrant who became one of the most admired Americans of the twentieth century. He created and owned NBC Radio, and in the 1940s he created the NBC television network.

He also owned the company that produced RCA Victor television sets. He created NBC TV so that people would have something to watch when they bought RCA Victor television sets.

Imagine the world after World War II; in the late 1940s and early 1950s we were at the top of the world, we were the winners over Hitler and his ideas, and we, as GIs and as a nation, were admired and respected as few people or nations in history have been. We had saved the civilized world from an uncivilized nightmare that might have become the future of humankind were it not for the United States of America and its allies, the Russians, the British, and others. We were at peace, at great sacrifice, and though the world was still a turbulent place, America was different, and held in real affection by millions of people around the world.

Now imagine buying Sarnoff's RCA Victor TV set. It was a new technology, and no one was capable of seeing how powerful it would be. Within a few years, we were happily hooked on the delivery of images of fantasy and reality, entertainment and current events.

No one realized how hooked we were until we began to study the phenomenon closely and discovered that the American people's toilets, in the millions, were flushing at regular intervals, timed to the commercials of *I Love Lucy* and the breaks from the reality/drama of the Army–McCarthy hearings, broadcast live into our homes. Timing to commercial breaks was a perfect irony, because Sarnoff, the Immigrant Boy Who Made Good, was originally opposed to commercials on television. He thought that commercial television was inevitably going to create a shallow experience on NBC television, and CBS and ABC on that same RCA Victor television. We might have had more than one TV, each set dedicated to a different network. Might have been . . .

Now imagine turning off the TV and going to bed; imagine not knowing that when you turned off the RCA Victor TV that Sarnoff had sold you, it didn't go off. (That didn't happen; just imagine that it did.) It stayed on and listened and recorded everything it could, and sold the information it received to advertising.

Imagine finding out about that in a newspaper or on the radio or even from a television news bulletin. *Perhaps Sarnoff would deny it at first, but then he'd have to fess up.* So, add to his list of "hypothetical" ethical lapses (or criminal behavior): "Lying under Oath."

(Please remember this didn't happen, it's a story, a tale, IT DIDN'T HAPPEN . . .)

But imagine how we would feel about Sarnoff then. CBS and ABC didn't do this, only David Sarnoff's NBC (this is my story, remember?). Our society as a whole had heroes who were your neighbors and our GI fathers who just a minute ago had saved the world from Hitler; we watched *Leave It to Beaver* and Walt Disney shows, the world was still trying to comprehend the word "Holocaust," Ike was in the White House, boys were in Cub Scouts, and America was the most admired country on the planet. What would we want to do to Sarnoff for being revealed as a snaky con man, worse than Bernie Madoff, for damaging our fine reputation in the eyes of the world?

We'd be thinking thoughts that are fear and anger and stuff not fit for polite society.

WE'D WANT TO STRING HIM UP BY HIS THUMBS, wouldn't we?

WE'D WANT TO SEND HIM UP THE RIVER, wouldn't we?

You betcha.

So, now, Mark Zuckerberg . . .

Zuckerberg isn't nervously rubbing his thumbs while he appears on the news under oath in front of Congress, is he? I bet he isn't even worried about any kind of punishment at all. And we don't expect any, do we? Even when the owner of Facebook announces that he is going to allow a change of rules and says he will encourage Facebook's users to assassinate Putin, a stretch of what we would call appropriate behavior . . .

What changed?

I mean, aside from a new technology, what changed?

We did.

That's what this book is about.

One Thought Scares Me...

**We Teach Our Children
What We Wish Them to Know;
We Don't Teach Our Children
What We Don't Wish Them to Know**

Chapter 1

A Spiral of Decay

I'm not a tease, so here it is in one sentence: If we share the sovereign's power but no one tells us what that means and how that works, then we don't got it.

We don't teach our Constitution anymore.

We don't teach our Bill of Rights.

We don't teach our governance theory, thought to be at the time of its creation the most radical theory because no other country agreed with our idea that Sovereign Power could be left in the hands of all of the people. We call the study of government and the tools necessary for the maintenance of a civil society "civics."

We don't teach civics either.

All these things have been removed from American public schools for over fifty years.

Have you felt the consequences of what I just told you? Does it explain a large part of the spiral of decay we all feel in the country today?

Does it make you angry? Does it horrify anyone, other than me? Because it's horrifying, people. This is our one real world, and it has become unquestionably absurd and suicidal. We were the first to attempt a sensible approach to create fairness in governance. We could have done much better, but at least we didn't just repeat the structures of governance that had preceded ours, all having built-in advantage for the Few, keeping the rest of us, the Majority, as cattle.

We believed that educating "the cattle" turned them into humans who created the first true civil society. No other country allowed sharing the power of the sovereign with other sectors of society. The aristocracy, the church, the poor—none had power that had not been granted to them by the King. We fired the King for fraud when we defeated the British in war. We found ourselves having the freedom to create new paths, which we had just then learned from Scots professors enamored with the philosophy called the Enlightenment.

Our obligation was to pass on what we learned from generation to generation.

That was the deal, and then we broke it. We broke the deal that we had sworn never to break, for no reason I can think of as worthy.

Does that *anger* you?

It is especially absurd to think our children could run this complex country without learning anything about its government first. We can't fly a plane without training, or practice medicine without attending medical school; then explain how we can send people to Congress who haven't first learned the workings of government or what powers the Congress has. It's not really enough to say, "I'll learn it once I'm elected." Sounds wasteful, costly, and fundamentally antidemocratic. Why? **Because not teaching civility and the core values of the Enlightenment philosophy that underpin our Constitution and our Bill of Rights is not just brainless but a black hole that sucks intelligent life down and gone.**

Seventy-five years ago we were among the most admired nations in the world, the only one respected for all the right reasons. **We were never perfect**—the most important political revolution in the history of civilization wasn't perfect, let alone the operating manual to run it, and the rights and liberties and responsibilities we laid out to humanity in those founding documents might have been better stated.

But our imperfect political miracle changed humankind for the better. We freed an enormous majority of people from an existence that had been an unbroken shriek of pain, punishment, and enforced ignorance; we brought true power sharing between the secular world of geopolitics and the moral world of spiritual progress closer to one another than had ever been thought possible or sane. We attached the goals of our Revolutionary Doctrine to real utility: the firing of monarchy for fraud, the spreading of the sovereign's power through all the former castes and classes, the unity of all our founding documents being bound by the philosophy of the Enlightenment. Those documents told us and the rest of the world **who we are** and **why we are who we are**, and who we intended to be—which meant different and better than any other nation. More inclusive. More generous. More rooted in the common people. We made a promise to educate our public, including our poor, in their preparation in learning how to run the country or whatever endeavor they chose. Then we stopped. We stopped teaching any of these classes, without announcement or any public discussion. These classes separated us from all other

countries, created intellectual creativity and musculature, unlocked the shackles that had tied us to
enforced ignorance since the beginning of recorded
history, so it was a **big deal**—and deserved headlines,
investigations, protests—and got silence.

Now if we're very, very, very lucky, it won't be too
late to revive the essence of what America did, what
Americans were and can still be, if they have the
courage and intellect and spirit to stop the bickering of the infantilized grown-ups who are presently
the shameful ruling generation. The fools who inhab-
it our power structures, our courts, our information
industry, our school boards—they refuse to see what
is right in front of us all, refuse to practice the
ideas that made America great and which are still
believed in by millions around the world, and which
are, to my bitter regret, scoffed at by our own.

Contemporary America is a tragedy because we have
obscured the essence of our civil society and let the
meaning of America be reduced to guesswork. **Who we
are** and **why we are who we are** was stolen from us, and
the scene of the crime was *not* surrounded by yellow
police tape. That made it difficult to tell anyone
where the crime took place, or if a crime had in fact
happened.

The thieves were very smart, very patient. They
started by taking only enough to make us lose our
way, and then apparently got mean drunk and began
removing anything they could carry, until they'd left
a stripped and empty schoolhouse, unable to teach
anything meaningful, anything based on the most generous philosophy ever conceived in the secular world.
We rid ourselves of kings and put our faith in
the people, spreading sovereign power among all. It
worked like a dream, until we stole the teaching of

the Constitution, and the birth-tale of the nation, and the civic tools that allowed for intelligence to become creative, stole the ability to learn when we stopped teaching any of this to our own children. We lost faith in ourselves and the values and the virtues that brought us so far.

Faith is not something you lose overnight. You believe, and you speak from your heart the words that reflect that belief. You're sustained by your belief, and the words celebrate what faith gives you. Then one day you realize that the words and the rituals of your faith have become only words, the rituals empty. And can you even remember what caused your doubts, or when your faith fled?

Faith in what, exactly?

Well, faith that the institutions of America were ours. Faith that we were all on the same team. Or that the machinery of the American idea, the machinery of republican democracy, was manageable. That it wasn't a sham. That our future was inevitably better.

We had changed in any case. We had at least exchanged one worldview for another. The filter through which we have perceived the world has always been self-confident, perhaps misguided at times but so be it. We have believed in ourselves and our abilities.

Now our filter is different, and we have no such confident worldview. We have no faith in our abilities. We have no connection to the future. Our faith in our future is shaken, because our belief in ourselves is rocky. **We have lost our faith in the powers that brought us this far—the powers of will, imagination, effort, and community.**

So what are America's fundamental constitutional values? Which values come from family? Or your religion? Which values come from tradition? Why do we assume America today actually agrees with the Constitution and its Bill of Rights? How do you even know? *It has not been studied in over fifty years.*

Most Americans can't answer that question, because we simply don't know enough anymore. We should be able to answer that question, and were able for the longest time, but not the last fifty years. That's how long the study of the Constitution has been absent, as well as the study of the governance structure the world once knew as revolutionary, and the capabilities of a civil society, the musculature we get from opposing views, the opportunity to have opportunity, and all the rest we pretend to know but don't.

Will Durant, who was among the most respected historians since the discovery of the New World, said that "history is to a nation what memory is to an individual. . . . Without memory a person is unknowable to himself and anyone else." Remove a nation's history, and that nation becomes disconnected and drifts away like an enormous balloon that escapes from the Macy's Thanksgiving Day parade, floating away slowly enough to be recaptured if the nation just thought it important enough.

Are the children of today and the time to come capable of running America when they are called to do so?

No. No, they're not.

Anyone paying attention over the last decades might have realized that we have become passive rather than active, that we watch politics the way people slow down to view a terrible car accident, hoping to see blood and brains and suffering, but never thinking we might offer up any help, any idea, any activity that could alleviate any pain.

This is no accident. This is somebody's fault. People in power, bought people, people in positions who can harm the public body through ignorance and treachery. The people who put them there.

You.

You who are reading this. You may deny it; that's what you're good at. But it doesn't change the fact that you—as parents, as citizens, as politicians—did this stupid and horrible thing. And you continue to do it even as you read this book.

I can imagine that some of you might be put off by my tone, but my tone is appropriate, better than the silence that usually surrounds this issue, better than the calm lies that mislead, and far better than the America that has resulted from the false discussions we have pretended to have. If you are already aware that turning students into citizens is the main reason for public education, then you are as rare as moon rock. Let me remind you that we have denied you and your children, even your parents, the Constitution, the Enlightenment philosophy, and the birth tale of our country. We've also denied you debate, civility, and clarity of thought.

I am not a cynic, despite what some people may believe. Nor do I belong to the "gaggle of Hollywood Liberals."

I will say two things:

I gaggle for no one.

And I am, if anyone bothers to ask or listen, a "Lib-o-Conserve-o-Rad-o-Middle of the road-o." I have been for many years, as I bet most of you are. You just haven't thought about it enough lately.

I am neither a scholar nor an academic. You will not get footnotes or lists of books that influenced me. I just read history, all the time, history of the British, the Chinese, the Mongols, the American Civil War, every point of view from Thomas Keneally to Gore Vidal. I love reading authors with opposing views. And I didn't take notes because I was reading for pleasure, not in formal preparation for compiling a list such as academics insist on.

Most important, though, I am an American, which has meant (in the past at least) that I am entitled to my point of view, an opinion. It's having that opinion that gives me the right and obligation to write this book.

My message may contain mistakes in grammar and proper publishing etiquette. If I neglected to annotate or footnote, or chose not to, I apologize for those misdemeanors. However, I am correct in my content and my perceptions of the necessary place Civics holds in public schools. I also believe that anyone who opposes that statement is corrupt, evil, or lacking in basic intelligence.

If anyone aims their weapons at me by saying anything like "There's no problem" (which has been said), or "He's exaggerating" (which has been said), or "He doesn't know what he's talking about" (which has been said), or "It's being taken care of already" (I dare anyone to say it), then I will say "Balderdash. Phooey. Show me."

I have read American history since I was eight or nine years old, always finding shameful sins and always things that I was proud of. I am the result of all of that and my family history. I was born in 1947. I admit to being as in love with my country, with my country's ideas, now as I was at ten, eighteen, thirty, and forty-five. I have never believed that America was perfect, or that America was only the product of its worst, but that it remains proof of the human desire to be better. Yes, that I believe.

But some years into the new century, I only saw reflected a complete blindness toward what I perceived as an inarguable fact: No one feels any sense of loss at the absence of civics education. I have been speaking for thirty years about this danger. I have seen audiences become filled with outrage, and then watched as that outrage disappeared before they reached their cars.

America has become expert at distraction and denial in the past fifty years. We forgot that Civil Society was achieved by constancy, not devoting one semester to it and thinking we could check it off a list. A very few centuries ago our ancestors created an invention of the mind that was a triumph of moral progress in the secular world, only to drop it in our own time like a toy fire truck we thought we had outgrown and left at the top of the stairs. We tripped on it, tumbling down through decay, back to the deliberate cruelty of the handful of the few who wield power over a shackled and ignorant majority. It is an eerily familiar, even comfortable, fate we see ahead of us. It is not an inevitable fate, but one we choose.

We the People have held this pearl in our hands and thoughtlessly let it drop, and even as it falls away we are distracted to the point of denial that it has any value. Americans don't feel the loss of the greatest compliment ever given to people. I want my grandchildren to know that I at least tried to tell you of the horror that approaches and that they will have to live with. Whether you hate America or love America, whether your reasons are the best or the ugliest, can you guess what awaits your descendants if you don't wake up?

When America fails, WHAT THEN?

Don't keep reading without giving that question some real thought.

Or . . . are you honestly too distracted to give any meaningful time to the answer?

If so, our children are doomed to mediocrity.

Pleasant thought, isn't it?

For us to slip, to refuse to teach what is our obligation to teach, is suicidal, proof that a whole nation can lose its collective mind. Had we not stopped teaching our legacy, maybe we could have made impossible the specific decay of our time.

I have Cassandra's curse: I can see the future, and I'm not kidding. In Greek mythology, Cassandra was a Trojan princess who was the object of a crush on the part of Apollo, god of the Sun, who gifted her with the ability to see the future. But when Cassandra scorned him, he cursed her in his rage and, godlike in his perversity, pronounced that *no one would ever believe her.*

I got that.

I can see America's future with a certainty that enrages me and fills me with despair. We can only stop the worst by reclaiming the doctrines we began with. We must reject the senselessness of hiding from our young the revolutionary nature of the ideas that were so fundamentally different from all others at that time, like the difference between God and the Devil. If we refuse our obligation to reinvest ourselves with these radical ideals, we will be guilty of collusion in the crime of killing America. There may be a nation called the United States of America, but it won't be the America we have known or struggled to preserve and improve. It will be a fake America, a pretense we have been practicing for over the last fifty years.

A FULL HALF CENTURY . . . and no one noticed that we had stopped studying the Constitution? And haven't yet? Haven't you put together that it might have something to do with the rotten state of everything in America?

We have slipped lower in reading, writing, and basic math skills, and we deepened the general level of ignorance. By failing to reinforce the singular values that were so revolutionary at our birth, we have failed to prepare our young for excellence in any field. My generation is the first to have made it impossible to fulfill the American Dream, of passing on a better country to our kids than the one we inherited from our parents. We are guaranteeing failure in the businesses our families built over decades; they will be eaten alive by smarter competitors, just as we don't have a clue how to prevail militarily against new enemies. Public service, or politics, used to be a "noble calling," but not in the last fifty years. Public service has become the definition of inauthenticity.

This is a desperately important issue, but we treat it as a low-priority problem, one that is considered too complex to solve. In our modern world, that is code for "we don't think our kids are up to it." That is nonsense. Kids are smarter and tougher than that. It's that we don't teach them with any rigor. We patronize them. And we ignore history, which is what provides them and us with appropriate examples. All of it keeps hitting an obstacle our society seems to cherish above all: profit. We are not encouraged to pursue with any real passion any profession other than that which will lead to personal wealth. There are exceptions, of course, but the system now seems to have emptied the bin of other values.

Left to ourselves, we slice through one another and our kids, dealing out what Spartacus learned at gladiator school was "a slow kill." We wound their brains just effectively enough so that they begin to drip potential, without feeling the steady flow of self-worth leaving them as the issues of the day are not explained in any detail. We read the reviews, buy the book, but never read the book. We read only the headlines; we don't read the whole article. We all just repeat headlines in growing frenzies of rage, never realizing that we are doing to others what we don't want others to do unto us, never realizing that over the course of our lives the steady invisible loss of intellectual creativity creates a loss of self-esteem. That in turn hardens into inarguable positions and impatience with other opinions, masking an anxiety about the tricky thought that "thinking is making my head hurt." No one is trained in how to find things out, and we just experience the confusion of the real world as "I must be stupid."

Doctors call conditions like bad blood pressure or hypertension "invisible killers." Not thinking will, without careful attention, kill you, or it will kill your brain and you will become—to use the medical term—"stupid." We say stupid things, we are angered for stupid reasons, we talk stupid, vote stupid, eat stupid, hate stupid, and don't have the slightest idea how to love ourselves or someone else. We aim our rifle at the wrong guy on the wrong battlefield. We vote to enrich those who are already billionaires, somehow thinking we are not punishing ourselves.

Our children are our future, and we have left them uneducated and unprepared. There's a legacy, don't you think?

Chapter 2

Why Civics?

The human brain is the most powerful tool in the universe, but it comes without an operating manual.
—BUCKMINSTER FULLER, *OPERATING MANUAL FOR SPACESHIP EARTH*

The brain of a human being is almost impossible to describe in the enormity of its capabilities, its power to take in information and factor that new information into greater, more capable abilities.

Brains that have been cut off from outside knowledge become dull in imagination, creativity, and comprehension. If it's true that one learns by example, humans with those types of brains will not be capable of seeing or choosing or understanding.

Take the word "example."

It means a thing that can be seen or understood as a model for something, as a learning aid, or as an illustration supporting something.

And the word "exemplify" means using an example to illustrate or understand or support a thing.

"Communication" is the successful ability to exchange ideas or thoughts with others, either through devices or talents that can reach others and articulate with clarity the detail of that which one wishes to convey. As exemplified by telephones or persuasion.

Take the word "endorse." To endorse is to publicly choose an idea, principle, or person, thus making it attractive, substantive, worthy, or necessary. As exemplified by agreement or support.

"Civility" is a controlled style of communication of opinions or ideas that allows all sides to remain respectful while assuring that the detailed differences between them are fully expressed, as exemplified by the comparison between rudeness and politeness. Surprisingly, we could learn from the old country, where civil discourse is illustrated in the behavior rooted in the ancient rules of the English Parliament. No matter how pointed the debates get, MPs precede statements to members with opposing views with the words "My Right Honorable Opponent." One can feel the insistence on respect, which requires clarity of thought and the acceptance of mutual respect maintained through imposed politeness.

Civility is not politeness or, even worse, an antique formula of polite words without purpose. *It is the oxygen that is required for survival in any republican democracy. Without it we strangle and die, as our republican democracy is dying.*

If we don't teach civility, and by example, we won't know it exists, even if we stumble on it in the dark. We won't know it for what it is, a tool that offers an alternative way to communicate that doesn't have built-in acceleration toward antagonism. Antagonism always misleads and causes one to potentially lose control.

So, if American children are not told that the people are the ones who have final **civic authority** in our system of Governance, if no one tells them what that means or how that works, if no one tells them they've got it, they ain't got it.

"Civics" is a boring word. There, I said it first, so don't bring it up again. But that's just the *word*.

We use the word Civics to cover the study of government, the concept of governance, which had to be learned by those who would in some form or other participate in running this nation. Civics is among other things the study of the birth of America, how we came to be a nation, and the invention of a doctrine of governance radically different than that of any other nation or empire in the world.

The achievement of a civil society, a manner of living that strives to include as few terrible things as possible, is a long epic tale that might begin in Eden. Historically it is all cannons and daring, courage and cowardice, genius and ignorance, inspiration and invention, terror and contempt, astonishing nobility and rapacious nobles, intelligence depraved, and too often chicanery elevated. Exploring that history is like watching a great movie, like Eastwood's *The Unforgiven* or Spielberg's *Schindler's List* or some other great film that I wasn't in. It is a tale so riveting you wouldn't want to get out of your seat to go to the bathroom.

Certain ideas have their time in the sun when they are new or nearly so. The philosophers of the Enlightenment era, the "influencers" of that century, let their opinions be known, picked over, approved of or not, accepted or adapted or rejected. A new opinion or belief may take hold in large segments of humanity and stay for a meaningful amount of time, long enough to effect changes in some important areas—like which god or gods to worship, or whether societies were immutable and unchanging or, like the Enlightenment

philosophy itself, a reflection of change or progress. Enlightenment philosophy caused extraordinary
upheavals in virtues and values, in perceptions of
self-worth, in the structures of classes, and although
revolutionary change was constantly being declared
done and dead, it had a surprisingly strong resistance and endurance, because the majority of people
had the most to gain. Too many people could see the
possibility of enhancing their lives in measurable
ways.

America has gifted the world with many things,
not the least of which was the right to talk politics in a normal tone of voice and *not be whispering*.
This may not seem like much, but it is much, and was
unheard of in the pre-Enlightenment world without
risk of losing a finger, a hand, or even your head.
Favoring some kind of change was more often than not
interpreted as violence, revolution, assassination,
or being an enemy of the state. And too often, it was
a direct path to death. But that was Europe.

In America, no one was afraid of talking politics.

Chapter 3

America Has Meaning

The people of America are the highest sovereign power in the world.

It's easy to forget the enormity of that statement. But America was the first nation to create a system of government based on the ideas of the philosophers of the Enlightenment, "loony extremists" who actually allowed for the opening of the gates to true political power to all classes. America explicitly addressed all those who had never come close to such things in the past—the unread, the untaught, those at the bottom of the barrel—and promised to give them the power once reserved only for kings. At its founding the United States was the only nation to lay out in writing the freedoms and responsibilities of citizens and the boundaries of the power of the state and to make them public for all the world to see. We are alone in having written, signed, and placed on a central, unavoidable wall a document that has made

our country respected and admired in saying to the
whole world:

"This is who we wish to be."

And because we are a work in progress:

"This is who we wish to be when we grow up."

It is undeniable that we have pursued those principles with mixed results. By any standard of prior
human behavior, however, it is also undeniable that,
while we have committed many of the same sins as the
rest of humankind, we have done immeasurable good as
well. America has illustrated the potential of humanity by forging a better way of life than any nation
before. No other nation had even the tiniest bit of
the ambition and respect for others that we drilled
into our youngest.

Just imagine how "the powers that were" must have
felt when they first read our Constitution. America's
system wove into the basic fabric of our government
restraints on that government, while at the same time
protecting us from the possible mass hysteria of pure
democracy. It gave the majority a veto power over
their representatives and over the special interests
that sought special favor. Our radical theory was
based on a thought experiment never actualized until
us:

*The Ruler and the Ruled could come from the same
place.*

America had declared war against the ways of the
whole world. That was an attack leveled and sustained
against the basic structure of societies everywhere
in the eighteenth century. If they could, the rulers
of that world would have enthusiastically come over
here and strangled us in our beds. Alas . . .

We said that common people, with a basic education of the ability to read, write, do sums, and
learn the actual difference between the governmental

structures they'd come from and the different values of America's specific governance structure, could have a banquet of rights and liberties and responsibilities, including participating in running the government if they chose. They didn't have to, but the option was theirs.

Government of the people means **OF** the people.

Government for the people means **FOR** the people.

To make sure there was no misunderstanding and it was not a sham transfer of power, but real, we spelled it out . . .

Government was meant to be **BY** the people.

Not by those who attended university, nor the wealthy, nor the nobility, nor a king, because we didn't ennoble anyone. Not the religious, either, because we made it such a crucial point that religious faith was a personal choice, not a public requirement.

The world may point fingers at us each time we fail our public aspirations, but they can only admire our audacious bravery for making those aspirations known. They know that each time we succeed, we are fulfilling the mandate that gives America *meaning*. Not every country has meaning, but we are famous for ours. It caused the largest voluntary mass movement of people in human history because we pronounced our values to a world whose nations denied those very values to their own. This is why people wanted to come here throughout our history, and still do.

Peoples from around the world, regardless of gender or color or the strangeness of their gods, came here knowing that America would teach them to read and write and do sums, teach whatever it took to make them as American as they must be. Teach them to read for themselves the Constitution, instead of just hearing about it. We said that civic participation

was open to all. That children of the least among us
could run for political office, even president. When
relatives back home found out that those who left
earlier were mayors or policemen, they got ready to
go. They had found "the city on the hill" and wanted
their piece of it.

We didn't set out to cause a worldwide revolution,
but we did it regardless. People around the world
don't say, "I can't wait to get to Kenya" or "Brazil"
or "Iran" or anywhere else. They say they can't wait
to get to America, because "America" has meaning in
this world.

Our founders made a deal with the world's poor,
whom we invited to this country where they would work
hard and receive freedom, responsibilities, education, and opportunity, enough so they could actually
run this country.

We are not keeping that promise.

Many Americans no longer want to provide a safe
haven for the world's poor and desperate. We express
anger toward and hatred of those who are doing exactly as our families did. We have stopped equipping new
arrivals with the fundamentals all of them must have
if they are meant to work for the country or run the
nation in the future, to design the civil society we
all want for our children's children.

We the People are meant to be the most formidable
power. It's not that one citizen can be as powerful
as one monarch; it is that the majority, equipped
with civic tools and a civic education, can unite and
attain a greater power than any monarch or autocrat.
Civic knowledge allows us to point out the important differences between our form of government and
all others. It allows us to name the betrayers who
have twisted the promise to the point of disfigure-
ment, each victory by corruption or narrow-minded

self-interest weakening us and leaving us farther away from our better angels. The authors of the Constitution always saw the benefit in teaching the untaught about America's enlightened principles, whether it was on days of national celebration or later in public school. The more you know of our system and the values it stands for, the better Americans you can be. All of us understood that until we got too smart for our own good.

Chapter 4

A Shared Foundation

All of us have power defined in the Constitution, and that is what has been taken from us. If you graduated from high school any time approximately between 1975 and today, participatory citizenship was no longer among the goals you had been taught to perpetuate our revolutionary idea. You are therefore different from the generations that came before you, because those generations knew the achievement of the Constitution and the Bill of Rights were not an accident of history.

It was the acknowledged intention of those who invented America.

Although it took some time for the national and local governments to recognize the obligation to pass it on, by the early twentieth century American students in public schools began a superb civic education; they studied the Constitution, the circumstances that created it, and the supporting materials needed to comprehend it. They were taught enough to know enough to participate in running the government and the society our founding documents created. And all this was part of the earliest public school grades, not kept until the end of high school, or withheld until university. It was taught as the method in all classes, from science to history and from as many angles as possible. We learned Civics before we knew we were learning Civics.

Public school years are not meant to be years of acquiring expertise, but the time for shared foundations to be laid. It's not necessary by the end of public school to understand the highest of mathematical thought, or to know every instance of scientific advance, but to use those years to introduce the shared basics.

They are not now so taught.

Nor is government. Not our government.

Nor is logic or reason.

So why have we ceased to teach these subjects, to understand or defend them?

Or did you even know that we'd stopped?

We are not fools; we are able to undertake the serious business of governance if we train ourselves to its necessities. We do not lack common sense, but we need education to understand governance, as lawyers or doctors need education to understand medicine or the law. These things are not transmitted in the blood or the atmosphere; they must be taught, as the Ten Commandments are taught. Some actually believe that man is born with some sense of moral justice, but even they know that without clear instruction, that inborn morality is not enough to reach the level or attain the detail of the Ten Commandments. Morality precedes the directives of Judaism, or Islam, or

Christianity, but also is shaped by training. Moral codes are the result of guidance and learning.

So, why would anyone believe that the political rights and boundaries described by our Constitution and Bill of Rights need not be taught? The authors who wrote the tracts and plays and pamphlets that were the foundation of Enlightenment thinking are not part of any grade school curriculum anywhere. They are the starting points for the intricate history of norms that all Americans should become familiar with, and just as in medicine, law, or science, early education should teach the shared foundational tools of good citizenship.

There is no law that says you have to be smart to run the government of America, but common sense tells us that smart is better than stupid. Further, participating in sovereign power requires being an informed voter, to know enough about the workings of governance to fulfill the mandate. You learn what kind of nation you live in, what the maintenance of republican democracy requires; you give it musculature with agility of mind and clarity of thought.

The logic of education can be laid out quite logically. Guiding students to become citizens begins with simple ideas and then proceeds to more and more complex ones, to help them discover, develop, and think with growing confidence, improving clarity of thought and clarity of expression until they are second nature.

Our common sense tells us that even if you never choose to participate in government, you can still comprehend how the laws passed by others affect your business, your taxes, and your family life. Common sense can tell you what is sensible for a particular time and place and what priorities are first or last, but it is only a starting point. What is common sense in one place might be the dumbest thing you could do in another.

In London in 1776, you could be standing on a corner looking in a window to evaluate the clothes you must buy, taking into consideration that this purchase must last a year, when you hear the sound of hooves on cobblestones, wheels and a carriage approaching you. Common sense then and there tells you whoever is in that carriage is wealthier than you, so you take a step back and lift your new hat in respect, avoiding the puddles that would ruin your handsome new shoes. Common sense tells you you've done the right thing, and changing your respectful tone to one aggrieved will not serve you. Local knowledge, needs, customs, and traditions all inform common sense.

We must keep this in mind when providing an education for our children. Don't lie to them or baby them. Prepare them for reality, rather than telling them that they're never wrong, that they deserve special treatment, or that getting rich should be their only goal in life. If you create pride in the hearts of your children when you tell them of your nation's stories, don't forget to give them the best reasons to love their country. Don't tell them we're "exceptional" unless you can tell them why in realistic terms. We are not exceptional simply because of divine providence, or because of our military prowess, or because we are south of Canada. *It's because we freed the intellect of the human race and rewarded mankind with freedoms and responsibilities once reserved only for kings and dukes.*

The intellect that won the war against the mother country, designed the Constitution, and created a republic to allow for democracy could have been smarter. It didn't occur to us right away that we, as a society, should be responsible for maintaining schools that taught the new basics, such as the ability to read the document we were so proud of or to cultivate the tools of reason and communication that are essential to slowing the pace of governance, so that outbursts of mobocracy did not wreck the democracy that living in a representative republic made possible.

But over the course of our first century, we established the public school system. For two hundred years, we used our birth tale to give us pride, to shape the minds of our children, and to create a civil society. America justifiably had bragging rights. We were determined to create a resource pool from which would come those who chose a political career—or careers in business or the professions or the trades—and those who didn't. There would be a fair and equal starting point, which had never existed ever. Anywhere. Anytime. (Though the latest idea, that there should be a guarantee of success at the conclusion, turns life into a mere performance, without risk or challenge.)

At the birth of our country, our leaders insisted that education for the citizenry was not just a right but an obligation, which in itself was a revolutionary doctrine. We ennobled no one, trusting that Americans would admire merit over bloodline. The idea that immigrants, new Americans, could be given an equal opportunity to learn all they could for any purpose they might choose was a compliment and a belief that struck the perfect opening chord. The first schools founded during the colonial period were created by churches, but by the eighteenth century education was supposed to not only build character but also teach practical skills and civic responsibility. Parents wanted their children to have those virtues, and strove to pass them on to their young at home, in churches, and in schools, especially on days of national celebration like the Fourth of July and Washington's birthday. Turning a passive citizen into an active one was never left to chance.

While the nation sought to enhance sovereignty for the citizenry by advancing education, the idea that the federal government should help pay for establishing schools wasn't realized for a century. Public education was strictly a local matter. Especially in the countryside, many Americans received their civics education through our election system. The mountain came to Muhammad. Campaigning became highbrow entertainment, though not comparable to today's politics as entertainment and shallow distraction. In our early years substance was held in the highest regard. Candidates would travel from town to town to make speeches and engage in debates. Those who sought careers in politics made their reputations as orators elaborating on the singular uniqueness of our republic or attacking the issues of the moment, while entire villages, young and old, listened and learned.

American towns and villages would hear and be persuaded by oratory and rhetoric. Both were talents to be prized. Mastery of both would send men to Congress. The expansion of the brain in sums, in law, in all subjects, would allow for the public to be smarter and create resource pools from which we could take those who pursued politics or school teaching or pastry making.

By the time the national government accepted the responsibility of public money for public schools, civics had become the catch-all name for the basic tools that all citizens needed. Civics taught us how to be good neighbors, good townspeople, and good politicians. These tools created what we call a public sphere, where people of different backgrounds, status, and class found common methods of communication and could learn sovereign power.

These shared tools of a thoughtful nation tied the newer Americans to older Americans, German Americans to Italian Americans to Chinese Americans, Christians to Jews to . . . You all know this song, not one of you hasn't heard it; you just haven't had it in your daily lives for so long that it sounds like a set piece of antique clichés, which it is not. We became the engine of the most productive society ever known, which eventually made us among the most admired countries in history.

America is more than a nation; it is a state of mind that is optimistic and willing to take risks. It is a work in progress that has unfortunately frequently taken steps backward, ignored sins as big as our soul, but attempted from its inception to lean on the belief that the potential of the least among us was to be cultivated and made capable; and that we could prevail, on the basis of that one assumption.

By not teaching all that we have stopped teaching, we have returned to a time of senselessness. We defied all the storms that history could throw at us, and we prevailed. Can we prevail against the big fat joke that we would just throw it all away for no damn good reason at all?

Are we more comfortable living in senselessness? Are we yearning for that ancient mistreatment, where we didn't have to think, where we knew the evil and our place as victims within it? The familiar boot on your neck once more?

In the modern world we have a name for the impact

of traumatic, extraordinary circumstances, what happens inside ourselves when ordinary people such as
you are held hostage, like in the movies when a bank
robbery goes bad and the hostages are abused, sometimes tortured, for so long that they become twisted
to the point where they fall in love with their cap-
tors. It's called the Stockholm Syndrome. It is grotesque, by any definition of that word. It resembles
humanity's response to its treatment by the ruling
classes for the entirety of human civilization.

Chapter 5

The Few versus the Many

Without exception, all who came here shared one thing: **They all came from somewhere worse.** Everywhere else the poor of the world were treated like cattle, and had been throughout all of history. The wealthy and powerful never came here. Why would they? They were doing fine where they were.

The world was for the Few. The few reaped all benefits, exercised all power, enjoyed all pleasures.

Until us.

Wherever you choose to start looking, before Ur and Mesopotamia, before Abraham, Brahma, or Lao-Tze, from before Pharaonic Egypt and Alexander the Great, through all mankind's the world's empires and nations without a break, this was the ugly truth of the world:

"You are a serf.

Your grandchildren will be serfs.

And my boot will always be on your neck."

Until us.

That world was a misery, a planet spinning through space "where no one can hear you scream," with poverty and suffering the only constants, day and night. The religions of mankind were culpable for enabling the continuation of torture, enforced ignorance, and fear. Look back and see no one who could call out the powers that were, except for the rarest and most inconsistent of spiritual radicals, who were usually killed early enough so that their revolutionary influence would be immediately diluted. That is even true of early Christianity: Neither Peter nor Paul nor John nor Mary could even agree about Jesus's true message as it might have applied to bettering the living circumstance of man or woman. Best to persuade them that however painful your circumstances of life, how bad your sins, if you held fast to the rules of kindness, generosity, and most of all forgiveness of those who mistreated you and yours (thus avoiding messy bloody revolts against those who were within striking distance), an eternity spent in the loving embrace of God would be yours.

A reward after *death* is as easy as the telling.

Think of the men who made up the armies of Alexander the Great, the Caesars, the Persian Empire, the Byzantines. Think of their wives and children. Think of the Chinese trapped within the Confucian order or the castes of India. Think of the czars and the monarchies of France and Spain, with their beliefs in Divine Right that precluded any authority that didn't come from the ruling sovereign by God's order. Or think of England . . . which no one did at that time, because that was where the "nuts" were grown.

Concerning every empire and nation in history, we learn of the leaders and their battles, the courtiers, the head priests, their aristocratic families and hangers-on. Yet how often do we stop and ask: Who were the soldiers in their armies, the sailors in their navies? What about their wives and children, who had no shelter from taxes and famine? Who was killing and being killed, raped, starved without pause? What percentage of the human race could enjoy any of the pleasures offered or escape the horrors that were far too easy to fall onto those at the bottom?

The few had pleasure, leisure, luxury. The many had fewer pleasures, fewer skills, and often fewer limbs.

Until us.

Read accounts of the wars between Sparta and Athens, or between Rome and Carthage, or the Gauls and Rome, or the Saxons and Danes, and you will read of armies of 50,000 or 100,000. Read of Napoleon and the leaders of ancient regimes who, desperate to end his political threat to them, fielded armies of millions to kill him. Sometimes I doubt those figures, but that's probably my wish. If they are real numbers, well then . . .

If real, we have had some hundreds of millions of people die in wars of no real import to them. Those who fought and died were lost to family, country, and thriving economies, to art, or progress, material or revelatory. Some survived and prevailed, were noticed by their god-king and patted, petted, had their names remembered for a time, though not for a length of time that really counted. But mankind has always been a quirky species, and some die, shrieking in horrible pain, but ecstatically happy in the knowledge that they would be remembered for a time as long as one intake of God's breath.

Sounds ridiculous, but there you are.

In the history of human civilization, one's brain was never a factor giving a poor man (let alone a woman) a chance of rising from the station he was born into. The poor were usually tied to a specific lord or estate, and that was that. Poverty was more than an economic condition; it was a paralytic. And it was a crime.

Dwell on that for a second. Poverty was a crime.

If you were poor and you wanted to learn to read or write to escape your poverty, you could be punished by imprisonment, fines, or having your nose chopped off. And that's just for asking.

Sometimes it does seem as if poverty brought out the worst in some people, and I'm not referring to the poor.

Sometime during the late eighteenth century, when glazed windows became common, they taxed windows.

Now, that just feels mean.

For argument purposes, let's say the Few were 10 percent (it wasn't that many, but let's say the ratio of the Few to the majority was one in ten). The Few had the privileges; the rest were without privilege, without any "Get Out of Jail Free" card. In the earliest legal codes, crimes were described in detail, as were their punishments. Theft, murder, and adultery were harshly punished, often by death. But not everyone was treated the same. The punishments applied to all, but the wealthy could buy their way out.

From ancient Babylon, Hammurabi's Code states, "If a man has destroyed the eye of a man of the gentleman class, they shall destroy his eye . . . If he has destroyed the eye of a commoner, he shall pay one mina of silver. If he has destroyed the eye of a gentleman's slave, he shall pay half the slave's price."

This was the algorithm for the Era of Kings. And as Marshall Davidson states in *The World in 10776*, "Oddly enough, the punishments meted out in ancient Mesopotamia were the same punishments meted out in the British Empire of 1776."

Until us.

The way the English maintained the biggest navy in the world was simple. Press gangs knocked out men in taverns. When they woke, they were on ships out at sea. They had no chance to say goodbye to family, employers, and friends. *It was the king's rule to kidnap his own subjects and force them into labor.* If they survived for the three years they were away, then they told their wives and children—and employers if they still had them—what had happened and where they'd been. Life was difficult on land as well. It was said that in England you couldn't tell the difference between a hospital and a debtors' prison.

We were among the first to realize the comedy of kings, and the childlike deference we gave to monarchs and their partners in crime, the aristocrats. If it's hanging you suffer for "stealing" a deer from the royal forest, to give your family something to eat, or for not bowing low enough as you pass "your betters"—though you know they are aristocrats because someone did someone else a favor hundreds of years ago and his descendants are still being rewarded—you either call it a comedy or you sharpen your ax.

The power behind royalty and aristocracy was the concentration of wealth. They had the money and thus the power to hire domestic armies and use them to terrorize their own populations. They were haunted, however, by a terrifying fear:

There is no moat deep enough,
Nor castle wall high enough,
To keep the people from crawling over
And eating you,
If they ever find out how badly you have fucked
them.

Each time the oppressed rose up against the insane cruelty of their masters, each time they won, they lost; because wherever they emerged they were still surrounded by the same few, ready to shackle them again.

But now a rumor, whispered
A destination?
Yes, a place that didn't repeat the cruelty of the past.
A place across the Atlantic that welcomed them
And encouraged them to rise.

Which is why the American Revolution so horrified the ruling classes of the world. With the Revolution, we fired the monarchy and aristocracy for fraud and handed out sovereign power to be spread among all classes. What had been was deliberately cruel and unfair; what could be, once the world knew of the document our founders created, was history's longest step forward for moral progress, incomparable.

We, the winners of a war for independence, went on to create a governance structure that was the first established anywhere with fundamental support for the potential of the poor. We handed them access to political power by removing the obstacles of class or caste that kept them from an education or holding public office. With the dismissal of monarchy and aristocracy, we had clearly earned the word "Revolutionary." Being eighteenth-century men, the Founders were not entirely free of that era's thinking or its views of mankind's capability, but they embraced the philosophy of the Enlightenment, which had faith in the value of education to enlarge human potential.

Those authors of the Constitution understood that the world's poor had never been taught how to read or write or do sums, a fact that guaranteed their inability to run a nation. Education could make citizens expert in any endeavor from holding public office to leading men into battle to play-acting to pottery. Remove all official impediments to advancement, they believed, and the risk of monarchy retaking political power would shrink to the size of a fur ball.

I believe in the most dramatic version of the narrative of how America came to be. It would be a mistake to think that there ever was a Golden Age in America's history, a time when everyone felt good and right about the country we lived in. But nothing that has happened during my lifetime, or anything I have learned about American history, including our flaws past and present, has caused me to lose my fascination with the political design we created. This is because I think of America as a work in progress, as I believe the Founders did—a nation with a deep commitment to bettering humanity, imperfect as that commitment has been. It was imperfect, yes, but a far more honest attempt to spread political power to more of its citizens than any previous nation or empire ever thought sane or possible.

We can only judge whether as a civilization we are standing still and only pretending to be improving our moral and secular progress when faced with the history that brings the past into any kind of focus. Author and language expert Steven Pinker writes that humankind has clearly made such progress, but we blind ourselves because we are more comfortable dwelling on our sins than embracing real moral progress. I learned this in my own progression from the immaturity of drug use to the maturation process of drug rehab. It was there that I participated in exercises demonstrating that individually we so loathe ourselves that compliments can hurt like arrows and we immediately disparage any good feelings they might encourage. Our national history is the antidote for such self-destructive views, not by whitewashing but

by accepting the maxim "more knowledge, more power."
Our past is British, and studying that past lets us
see why it is so much easier to hate ourselves than
to take credit for our progress. It also demonstrates
how history can be forgotten, or transformed into
myth.

Chapter 6

The Tudors

Things changed with the Tudors (a family of ne'er-do-wells), who were mostly France-dwelling English who killed a king, Richard of York, and then slaughtered any and all who had been his allies, or who had some bit of knowledge, an affection for the Yorks, or perhaps just an attitude that Henry Tudor didn't trust. Such people might cast doubt on Henry Tudor's 1/32nd part of the necessary bloodline or endorse the Yorkists' rightful claim. The Tudors were powerful enough to collect allegiances from some Great Houses, not many but enough for the British to see that constant warfare among the noble families meant more Death. Henry Tudor was strong and amoral enough to hold the crown long enough for the people of England, exhausted by the bloodletting of the War of the Roses, to allow the Tudors to rule. The final bloodletting destroyed all those who questioned how he gained power. It was a storm of Death.

Richard of York, known during his lifetime by his loyalty to his brother Edward, had devout supporters; the northern city of York put up a banner along the outer walls of the city that announced in large letters, "we are the true and loyal supporters of the true King Richard of York. And we dare you to come up here." Neither Henry VII nor VIII ever went north during their reigns because they knew that doing so would create an uprising they might not survive.

The smartest thing the Tudors did was hire a PR agent to encourage the people to like them and validate their claim to the throne. The agent was William Shakespeare, and he wrote so beautifully about Prince Hal and his fight for England that, in the words of a great Shakespearean scholar, "he invented England." Hal was a Lancaster, from the noble house that opposed the Yorks. I believe that Shakespeare made Richard III the perfect villain by giving him the character of Henry Tudor, and simply naming the monster "Richard."

The last Tudor, Elizabeth, decided that the Tudor line was tainted and should not survive her reign. So she never married, never bore a child that we know of, and after almost a century of gore and murder over religion and dynastic power gave her throne to James of Scotland, part tepid Catholic and part tepid Protestant, and the Tudors were finally consigned to history as part of England's work in progress. That history started with the murder of a true king, proceeded with terror, beheadings and quarterings and witch burning, and ended in the King James Bible.

If you aren't aware yet that history is where comedy is born and thrives, all you have to do is know the one word, primogeniture. It was apparently a thoughtful decision, made by those who thought they were thoughtful people, and it was used by many

countries, some all the way into the twentieth century.

These were families that had wealth enough to need
wills and children enough to worry about them killing
one another. They solved that problem with laws that
allowed only one heir, the eldest son, to inherit.
He got it all, however big IT was; and the other, or
others, got squat; nada; nothing. Unless the eldest
chose to share out of an affection that might exist
between siblings, there was no begging or whining,
and second sons were expected to go into the military
or the church, the father or brother promising to pay
for as good a rank as possible.

If you're not laughing, then you had a bad day.

I am describing another wack job. The British Army
was funded by enormous amounts of cash, the larger
the amount the higher the rank considered. Some very
stupid men became colonels, and some very very stupid
men became generals. (Read *The Reason Why*, the story
of the Charge of the Light Brigade, if you are interested in inarguably stupid military leaders. It will
make you laugh so hard you might swallow your tongue,
and you will feel rage and despair, and want to open
certain graves and throw a corpse or two into a bog.)

Second sons, however, sometimes balked at a life
in the church and had no feeling for the army or the
navy or for squabbling over scraps that might have
fallen from the dinner plates of older brothers.

Many sons of families got out as soon as possible,
not from the family but England, Europe, and thought
to give the New World a try. So it probably came as
no surprise to Europe that their nephews and cousins
across the Atlantic were thinking crazy thoughts,
they already thought a continent populated by second
sons and their sons and daughters, their relatives
across the pond, were dumb as ducks.

Perhaps it explains why Americans won the war; I'm guessing that Lords Howe, Burgoyne, Cornwallis, et al. were lords or generals or admirals because they bought the ranks and believed they earned them. The British thought Americans were silly, which was the nub of it all, wasn't it? Which might have led the Brits to underestimate their American opponents, and shower us with contempt as we beat them at war, formed an alliance with Great Britain's eternal enemy France, and lost them their New World Empire; not being quick to learn, they continued their derision, scorning our political invention called the Constitution as having no substance, being silly at the core since their reliance on common people was the silliest thing they'd ever heard. It took them a century to finally credit our government structure with an agility they might have found valuable themselves, before feeling primogeniture bite them on their necks, and the siblings they had thrown away becoming Americans right in front of everybody. (As the French say, it is to laugh . . .)

It's kind of hard for us to see Great Britain as Europe saw it, which was an island of total lunacy. It was the place that one hesitated to visit because "There be monsters," not in the Atlantic but in London. In the centuries following the Tudors, many families sought peaceful lives in the New World where, once colleges were founded, Scottish professors taught them of the Enlightenment.

History is studied so the people of the present can be informed by their past in order to envision some sense of the future. It allows us to give our progeny a running start. Ignoring history is a clue to the senselessness that we have a proclivity for. It's why critical race theory is so controversial today. Not because it has any new information that disses whites; frankly, our racial and racist past has been taught as part of honest history for a long time. It just didn't go under the name "critical race theory." Opponents of an honest discussion about race are telling White America that Black America is trying to be better than whites, and that is not acceptable! No sir!

And it's also not true.

No matter how many times it has been said, too many white Christians have believed America was an exclusively white Christian nation, and everyone else had a guest pass. Scratch a conservative Christian with no Civic training, no knowledge of the Constitution or the philosophy of the Enlightenment, and you've got white Christians who seem to have no patience with all those who don't realize their guest passes have expired. Who cares how you are treated, they say; this is our country. All religions act this way, given a chance, which is one reason for all religions to be treated with the same respect, so one doesn't open country clubs advertising "no Jews, women or colored, except as waiters." There are still such places.

Deny Civics training to Jews or women or Icelanders, give them just enough power to abuse, and they too would open clubs denying entry to those who weren't on the charter committee:

"No Catholics, no Greenlanders."

Chapter 7

A Personal History

Every people has the right to know who they are.
And why they are who they are.

The Constitution is personal, to me, and you, and to all Americans. The tragedy is that so many fellow citizens don't know it, because they were never taught the Constitution, or the Declaration of Independence. Let me tell you a story. It's a personal story. I bet you have one too . . . because it is a story of America. The stories are all different, but together they make us a particular kind of nation.

There is a powerful history of political activism within my family.

I have the rare distinction of being able to say my great-aunt assassinated the Czar in 1881.

Helsya Helfman was a member of the Narodniki or Narodnaya Volya—"The Will of the People''—the group that assassinated Czar Alexander in 1881. Alexander Lenin, Nikolai Lenin's older brother, was in the group. The Okhrana, the Russian secret police, came down heavily on them. Most of the members were hanged pretty quickly. Alexander, who could have lived had he accepted the advantages his class offered, chose to be hanged. Fortunately for Helsya, even the Okhrana didn't hang pregnant women. Instead, my great-aunt was exiled and came to New York. All immigrants who came to America to be American had to register their names with a clerk on Ellis Island. If the names were too hard to say, the clerk changed them, and that was that. So Helsya became Elsie, and Helfman became Hoffman, and NEXT! So a young woman from Eastern Europe went into the building Helsya Helfman and out came Elsie Hoffman.

Ten years later her brother arrived. I don't know his name, so I call him Tevya. He was a pious man from a shtetl, and he got a job in the sanitation department. In those days, the garbagemen wore a kind of uniform: high boots, trousers stuffed into the boots, a wide belt like a dirndl, a blousy shirt, and a cap. As the story goes, Helsya wouldn't speak to her brother for ten years because "he wore the uniform of the state."

That's the story I grew up with, including the spelling of her name (some say it's "Hesya", others "Hessia", but I know her as Helsya). This story had floated around the family for years, taken as God's truth by some, scorned by others.

I have the good luck of also having two cousins, Gary and Robert Katzman, who are identical twins and both federal judges. We didn't meet until I was in my forties or fifties, but they turned out to be insanely great. Each were on courts right under the Supreme Court, but in different regions. When we met for the first time, we talked about all things family. Their mother was my father's mother's sister, still hale and hearty (knock-knock, still is). I asked if they knew of Helsya: Was she real? And really such a radical?

But they were from the other side of the family, not Elsie's, so it was a mystery to them both. But after I got home from that first lunch, both of them emailed me confirmation of Helsya and her involvement with the Narodnaya Volya.

There were two or three stories about Helsya after the assassinations. In one she'd been arrested and killed; in another she hadn't been killed, but the one I locked onto was the version that tied Helsya to Elsie. However, ten years later Wikipedia said she'd been killed by the Okhrana. I report this to you in the spirit of full disclosure and the sacred bond between writer and reader, but I don't buy the other artless crap versions for a minute.

My great-aunt's niece, my grandmother, was also called Elsie Hoffman. When my grandma Elsie was eleven, she was a witness to the Triangle Shirtwaist Factory fire, one of the great catastrophes during the immigrant wave that marked the end of the nineteenth century. One hundred fifty-four girls died, young women mainly from Eastern Europe with only the slightest beginning of a comfort in English. Like young ladies everywhere "of a certain age," they were thought to neglect their work with "too many cigarette breaks." At least that was the story the two owners of the sweatshop insisted on for locking from the outside the doors on the nineteenth floor to the fire escapes.

When the fire started, the women had no exit. They crowded the windowsills, breaking the glass for air, with the fire eating them from behind. The inevitable "curious onlookers" below watched the flames outline the trembling shapes, who "held hands and flew like birds," all the way down nineteen stories to the pavement. Their long Eastern European hair, their pride, aflame as they clasped each other's hands for

a last touch of life as they stepped out into the
emptiness in a last betrayal before the descent that
snuffed out the fire and their lives. What fast jour-
neys were theirs, from shtetl to America, and from
the nineteenth floor to the pavement. And no grandchildren at their feet to hear it told.

From where my grandmother stood, eleven-year-old
eyes fixed and wide, they looked, as they poised for
flight, like some grand fiery goddesses in triumph.
An image created by the burning of flesh and hair,
glowing with majesty, hair never to be cut into the
fashionable style of the time. Elsie caught every
detail—the wisps of smoke, the distant tinkling; she
saw the first feet, tentative and awkward, the women
like newborn fawns taking their first steps, but so
eerily understood to be so close to their last. Elsie
and the others, now joined by policemen and ambu-
lances, each unmoving and helpless, could see the
girls seeking the touch of each other, compelled by
the eternal companions of death—terror and love—
seeming to fly upward for a tiny second and then each
fiery goddess plunging down toward my grandmother,
each exchanging the light of the divine for the ashen
black of crows, crashing to my grandma's feet, piles
of human ruin heaped on one another's bodies. I can
imagine her expressionless face as she turned away.
According to family lore, Elsie went directly to the
Socialist Party HQ, where the tale ended with Elsie
Hoffman eventually becoming the private secretary of
Eugene Debs.

Do you know that name, Eugene Debs?

There's so much for you to know.

He was head of the Socialist Party and ran for
president as the Socialist candidate. He later spoke
against our entry into World War I, reminding people
that President Wilson had won his second term on

the promise, "I'll keep your sons out of this war." Debs made a speech urging resistance to the military draft. President Wilson had Debs arrested for breaking the Sedition Act, enacted a century earlier by John Adams, an author of the Constitution and second president of the United States. The Sedition Act made it a crime to speak against the government. Adams's version of free speech, I'm guessing.

Debs was sentenced to ten years in prison and disenfranchisement for the rest of his life. When he was being sentenced, he asked the judge for the right to speak. Receiving permission, he spoke for two hours. The speech ended with lines that have become large in history: "While there is a lower class, I am in it, and while there is a criminal class I am of it, and when there is still one soul in prison I am not free."

It was from prison that he ran for president and received close to one million votes, which was 3.4 percent of the total. This remains the all-time high for a Socialist Party candidate.

My grandma worked for him.

The two owners of the sweatshop on the nineteenth floor of Triangle Building were acquitted of any responsibility. Of course. But President Harding, a Republican who succeeded Wilson, freed Debs and gave him back his right to vote. Harding is known to historians as one of the worst presidents on all the polls that count that kind of shmoo. For me, freeing Debs elevates his reputation to one of the best presidents. It's my poll; I invented it, so go jump in the lake.

Throughout my life and career, political events have always demanded my attention as an American citizen, and I would sense Big Grandma gently, expectantly looking at me and waiting for me. And then I did . . . stuff . . . that would make her smile an approving smile. I am a potentially powerful person in my role as an American citizen. The Constitution tells me that, and so does Big Grandma Elsie.

I've always believed there was great art in the story of my family.

I am a "red diaper baby" and proud of it—the product of a society that was born just before the Great Depression from political radicals, exiles, communists, trade unionists, socialists, and anarchists. The men of my family and my neighbors, first in Brooklyn and then in Bayside Queens, New York, were all of the American Left, and they loved America like nobody's business. As I grew up in the 1950s, I knew that if you hadn't fought against Hitler twice, first in Spain in the Spanish Civil War and then again in World War II, you'd better have a damn good reason. Everybody I knew in my parents' circle were communists and socialists. My mother once said to me with great pride that she'd never voted for a winner. I asked her once why she was a socialist and not a communist and she said, "Better donuts."

My father passed away before I started to write this book. Our relationship was complicated, but I was very proud of his actions during the war. However, I couldn't tell him because I wasn't supposed to know about it. Well, not completely true; we did have one short exchange while I was in London. At this moment I don't know how much more I should say. Let's say that he had a war as violent as any movie, and leave it there, at least for now. And he was in the hospital for a bit more than two years.

My dad looked to me like a perfect nerd, with pictures from the 1930s showing big round glasses and trousers up to the armpits. He looked like "The Victim Personified." I had no clue that my dad was the leader of a Jewish gang, and fought Irish and Italian gangs. It was a terrible and violent way to grow up, and he never talked about that either.

During the war he had been sent to the University of North Carolina, where he was taught perfect German, being prepped to be part of the occupying army after the war. Henry Kissinger was in the same unit for a time. But Congress killed the school, and because they had taught him to speak German, they made him a scout and he found himself behind the German lines during the Battle of the Bulge.

The usual time in combat was twenty-one days. My father was sixty-nine days in combat, always behind the lines. His unit had one order: get info from an officer of the Wehrmacht. So they captured an officer, stripped him naked, tied him to a chair, and my dad would walk in with a bowie knife and say in German, "I'm Jewish."

I never heard any of this from my father, but my uncle and my mom told me, "Sometimes the guy didn't get out of the chair."

Which meant he'd been tortured to death. By the guy with the Bowie knife.

Still, Hollywood's vision of America helped sustain our European friends during the war. When the Nazis entered Paris, they told the movie theater owners that they had one week to play whatever films they wanted, and after that only German films would be allowed. Every theater in Paris played Mr. Smith Goes to Washington. True. When the occupation was lifted four years later, every theater in Paris played Mr. Smith Goes to Washington. True. (And if you don't know that film, you should be ashamed of yourself.)

Many around the world experienced fervent gratitude for America's existence during the dark Depression years of dictatorship that ended with the war, which were only a blink in our past. Joseph Stalin and Adolf Hitler were not thousands of years ago, but yesterday, and my father and his contemporaries fought Hitler to the death. My father's generation all knew they would all be killed if Nazism won, so they knew why they fought him: to protect not just our way of life but our lives.

There's a point I can't leave out, and the reason I started to tell this story. When my dad, fresh from the bloody turf wars of Brooklyn, left for a world war, he left with his local enemies, those Italian and Irish members of rival gangs. When they returned home, they all came back as Americans, every one of them. They had all given up the prewar bullshit and came home bound by the monstrous shared experience. Together, they lived on the same streets, shared in starting families, and only argued over politics. I never got to talk to my dad about any of this, but I bet he would have agreed with me. The bonding during that nightmare created Americans out of poor immigrant boys who grew up in the same fire, gave up childish things, and became American men.

I lived with them, I worshipped them, even when I disagreed with them politically. There are people who, like me, changed their politics from being "way over to the Left" to something else, but I never stopped to sneer at my former mentors. When I was nine I remember saying to my neighbor Tommy Grasso, a vet, "I get it! Your political psychopath is better than their political psychopath." And he laughed so hard he spit his milk up through his nose.

These were, and are now, the finest men I ever had the privilege to know, and though they yelled about Stalin "the Necessary" or Stalin "the Worst Monster Ever," like most Americans they knew very little about the Soviet Union. Their politics were never about foreign policy, but about domestic issues, like Nixon and the Committee, the Blacklist, and Premature Anti-Fascism. Their politics were always about the First Amendment. They had come to communism through the War against the Rich, from poverty and some protections like unions, and thought America was the beau ideal. These same men wept at Ebbets Field or Yankee Stadium when the national anthem was sung. When they heard me and my brother singing along, they would nudge one another and wipe the tears from their eyes.

Politics was meant to express different thoughts, and share them with others' thoughts. Now we don't teach what we share, and it would make all the difference. After fifty years of ignoring the beauty of the Bill of Rights, we should start learning that again.

Chapter 8

An Imperfect Miracle

In 2018, *The Atlantic* ran a series called "Is Democracy Dying?" The authors who responded all seemed to say "yes." Their response is echoed by even more pundits writing today. Many paint a grim picture for the United States, comparing it to countries of Eastern Europe like Hungary and Poland, where democracies are sliding back toward right-wing authoritarian rule.

I think these authors and pundits have forgotten a few critical things.

First, we don't live in a democracy.

We live in a republic.

We live in a republic that allows for democracy.

We pledge allegiance to a republic (or used to). The authors of the Constitution designed a representational republic because they feared pure democracy as much as they hated monarchy. They had witnessed spectacles of "mobocracy" and knew that people were

subject to occasional lapses we can call "the hysteria of crowds." Hamilton sneered at democracy as
it was then *perceived* and he wasn't entirely wrong.
Democracy was not the sheriff with the law on his
side. It was the crowd waking up to find a noose
in its bloody hands. This knowledge obligated the
members of the Constitutional Convention to seek a
creative solution to the transfer of sovereign power
from monarchs to the people of all the classes,
including the most common. They discovered the solution in the structure of the Republic, which built
in multiple barriers to thoughtless actions, making
room for deliberation, for thinking things through.
A Republic would allow for the People to be sovereign arbiters of political power by voting in and
out their representatives in state legislatures and
Congress. In the Constitution we make no mention of
monarchs, aristocracy, or churches. So who has sovereign power in America? General Motors? No. Silicon
Valley? No. The Fed? Nope.

The legal analysts who are experts in constitutional law all agree that the first three words of
the American Constitution make it crystal clear who
holds sovereign power in the phrase: WE THE PEOPLE.

Not some people, but all people. And the most
efficient way to reach All, and not just some, would
be through a public school system that reached more
students and offered to all the same study of government and the Enlightenment philosophy that was
the underpinning of the Constitution. And because of
its unique generosity and encouragement of all who
sought citizenship, it could be a strong basis for a
civil society.

Even though the basic structure of government
removed sovereignty from a monarch, many Americans

still shared the Old World's view that a passive and ignorant citizenry should be governed by an elite. The idea of the average citizen as sovereign was bitterly contested then, and still is by some wannabe aristos. Certainly some of those who signed the Constitution had their fingers crossed while signing; certainly some changed their minds after the signing was done. It is said that the genius of the Constitutional Convention was the creation of the Republic, which threaded the needle between minority rule and mobocracy. In other words, to repeat, the Republic allows for democracy.

If you look at the Constitution, at the description of the executive branch and what the presidency looks like today, you can see only one way for that enormous power to have been achieved. That is by politically creative men, who were caught by circumstance and proved willing to do what needed to be done to enlarge the executive's role. They didn't steal. They didn't hit us over the head or kidnap our kids and force us to give them more power.

Jefferson's response to the pirates of Tripoli is a perfect example. The Tripoli pirates appeared annually or biannually, demanding to be paid for using the waters that the pirates considered theirs. Although skeptical of one-man rule given the memory of monarchy and suspicious of a strong executive, Jefferson alone authorized the building of ships for a navy. The Congress was out of session; his was the only office open for business, so he alone approved the construction of an American navy, which he opposed on principle though he saw no alternative.

Decades later, faced with the unprecedented secession of southern states that dragged America into a civil war, Lincoln did what he had to do to preserve the Union. He was the most ridiculed president, not respected until he was dead. Most of his actions were also unprecedented, illegal, or the province of other branches of government. The Congress of the time was held tightly by the zealotry of the abolitionists, who wanted to treat the southern states as conquered provinces. Lincoln was constantly warned that he was acting in ways that were not constitutional, and was constantly threatened with impeachment. Lincoln answered as the brilliant lawyer he was: "The Constitution is not a suicide pact." And he proceeded to act outside its bounds in order to deal with the crisis at hand. No ifs, no ands, no buts.

So did FDR, so did Truman, and finally Trump. Oy vey—but four out of five ain't bad. The presidents who refused to govern, citing constitutional limitations, are considered some of the worst presidents in history: Van Buren, Tyler, Pierce, Buchanan. The Constitution also never guaranteed that Americans would always behave like good citizens. We had angry political divisions from the beginning. Especially in our first half century, congressmen even sometimes called one another out, challenging each other to duels. In 1856 Senator Charles Sumner of Massachusetts was attacked at his desk by South Carolina Representative Preston Brooks after a fiery antislavery speech. Brooks beat him with a cane until he was unable to rise. Brooks subsequently received as gifts canes from all over the South as a grotesque gesture of gratitude. Sumner could not resume his duties for three years. Sam Houston was also a senator at the time, and came to the floor wearing two loaded pistols, making it crystal clear he would shoot to kill anyone who crossed him. So Eastern Europe's struggling new democracies are not a smidge worse than we were. I guess those *Atlantic* writers overlooked this part of our history.

It took decades and a catastrophic civil war to settle the issue of slavery. Even then, for the next one hundred years, it was perfectly acceptable to pull over to the side of the road and hang a black man, which was done at the rate of about ninety a month . . . for a hundred years. You do the math.

Any attempt to stop such lynching was defeated by a coalition of northern and western politicians, who reasonably concluded that lynching was "an acceptable compromise" in the interests of national unity. Not until the Black Civil Rights movement hit television around 1960 did the whole country basically say, "*Ohmigod, what was that lynching thing?*"

It took us that long to learn that our political life could include African Americans (we haven't really learned that yet, but at least we have some guilt about it). Or that we as a nation might include women in any of this. Or that, as a nation, we should not have slaughtered the Native population. The entire idea that "all men are created equal" was and still is a central bickering point of our imperfect Constitution. The argument surrounding the Constitution comes down to this: Either it means what it says or it doesn't. I believe the Constitution means what it says. It is a work in progress.

America often claims exceptionalism, but it is not the only just, secure, and free nation in the world. Nor is it, as some would have it, somehow the favorite of divine providence. The history of civilization is strewn with nations and empires that thought they were "chosen." It amuses those who study history to find that the peoples so assured of their chosen status often end up fighting one another, trying to be heard above the din, to help providence get its aim right, but impossible to hear beneath the shouts of the blessed and the wailing of the dying.

Our country is not even exceptional in making its ideals a sustained reality. We pledge "liberty and justice for all," but in the due process of law justice is often as absent as it is present. Built right into our criminal justice system; our prosecutors are given promotion by the number of convictions they accrue, which tempts them to produce convictions rather than to see justice done. I'm not saying that all prosecutors behave that way, but the temptation is there. Kamala Harris was a prosecutor in California. Are there any questions we'd like to ask her? Some cases of injustice are notorious, and we now regularly see innocent people released from prison after spending decades there. The American justice system is too often a victim of men's natural self-interest and ambition. We punish the middle class and imprison the lower class, who fill the jails for street crimes, while the windowed suites in the cruise decks above us are filled with the happy feet of one of the worst criminal classes in history.

But no matter how badly our country has behaved, no matter how many sins we have committed or how often we fell short of our ideals, remember that those shameful acts were done in the midst of a battle fought between two ideas of America: the self-interest that can easily become greedy and sociopathic versus our better angels who openly declare for moral progress, generosity, and opportunity for all. No other country had this problem to the same degree, because most were already run by powerful monied interests, who saw no reason to create a better society.

Dismissing America because of its crimes overlooks so much that is uniquely good. In the age of its founding, no other nation strove to improve the chance of rising from poverty to anything better, to stop treating the majority of humanity as anything but cattle. Not in the entire history of human civilization.

America is a work in progress. Each group has had to "take a number and get in line" until they could command the proper attention. For some groups that line gets longer, and they have to wait longer than justice should permit, but we are as imperfect as the process we created. We will be judged for how well we overcome those imperfections, just as anything else we have created will be judged. "We"—as I intend it to be understood—means the all-inclusive "We," from the authors who created the American ideal to the assassins who are presently killing it, those who rightly deserve the long prison terms I yearn to give them.

So, yes, the Constitution is imperfect. It is not the be-all and end-all of everything. But it has a basic unifying fairness. We need to hold on to this, something larger, stronger, more central than us. It's a much more reliable thing than political parties. George Washington said, "The Constitution must always be central; the factions must always be peripheral."

Factions are political parties. At this moment we are living in the exactly opposite world, where our factions are central and our Constitution is peripheral. We are not focusing on anything we can share, only things that breed division. Parties are expressions of power, not principle. They have changed with the historical winds. The Democratic Party of 1860 was the party of slavery, of 1900 the party of Bryan and small farmers, of 1932 FDR's Working Man. Then in the 1960s the party of Black Civil Rights, and now the Party That Is Not Trump. The Republicans began as the party of Lincoln, then the party of Business, and then Business again and again, until Trump refashioned it in his image, which is beyond my ability to understand. Now it is Republicans who eagerly talk about a new civil war, and who embrace Confederate symbols and attitudes.

This is why America is so anxious, so weird, so angry and uneasy, so un-anchored. We are hitching ourselves to factions that could change and have changed, that can't be relied on to give us a common purpose. That can't be counted on to keep to the same principles from Tuesday to Wednesday. And that want—let's be honest grown-ups here—want the Constitution to remain peripheral, more and more, which means less and less relied on, and made meaningless even when mentioned in passing.

Teaching Civics is not a partisan thing more amenable for one party than another. Regardless of what members of the editorial board of the *Wall Street Journal* may say, did say, to me on the day I met with their board, there is no "hidden agenda" in the teaching of Civics to our young. That is balderdash and poppycock. It's a lie, meant to keep us from our birthright, born out of partisanship. There never has been a hidden agenda in teaching Civics; in fact it's always been the exact opposite. We proclaimed our promotion of a civil society to the world, even etched Emma Lazarus's poem "The New Colossus" on a plaque on the Statue of Liberty: *"Give me your tired, your poor, your huddled masses yearning to breathe free. The wretched refuse of your teeming shore. Send these, the homeless, tempest-tost to me. I lift my lamp beside the golden door!"*

But we have lost our ideals, and with them the civility that allowed American society to exist with many people of strongly held opposing religious, political, and social beliefs. To work together with an underlying unity. This is why we need to be reeducated about our founding principles and our history. We need to know the American story, and because we abandoned it, we broke the deal; we have no muscle memory of living with it. We have been distracted and derailed, *deliberately*, by those who have placed profit and self-interest above our better natures and really don't care about the consequences.

We have lost our common sense.

Which brings us to another critical error of *The Atlantic* authors and all those others who have declared that our democracy is dying. Our national birth tale and its world-shaking consequences have not been taught to our own children for fifty-plus years. We stopped teaching the fundamentals of the Constitution and the Bill of Rights and the values of the Enlightenment we built them on.

Those missing lessons would allow us to know who we are and who we are not. We cannot know America by magic or God's favor. We can only know it when it is taught to our young, so they grow up into active citizenship. Let our young study our founding documents as written, and the ideas that went into them, so we can then reverse the growing decay in our values of the past several years, and the decay of the most basic principle of Republican Democracy, which is the willingness to share political space with those with whom we disagree. The absence of Civics education is behind all the rage that accompanies our uncontrollable partisanship, which doesn't allow for the legitimacy of any views contrary to one's own. That in itself opposes the idea of America. We now see

the result of abandoning the teaching of those ideals and values in the 1980s, and the effect on the
generations schooled since then.

No wonder even our best thinkers can't get a han-
dle on what's wrong with America.

After more than two hundred years of knowing that
the teaching of certain ideas and principles was necessary, why did we suddenly stop and decide, "Nah, we
don't have to . . ."

Chapter 9

The James Dean Generation

I call them the James Dean Generation.

It's said that on the night after James Dean died in a car crash all of Sunset Boulevard was a sea of open leather jackets and white T-shirts, cigarettes hanging from fans' lips and tears running down their cheeks. They were mourning in homage to their hero who'd been so confused by mixed messages from all sides of the culture, who felt he'd had no mission, no purpose, and screamed, "You're tearing me apart!" They were children during the war, and they couldn't see the connection between Iwo Jima and Dad's present pursuit of suburban blah, played by Jim Backus in *Rebel Without a Cause*. They sought purpose and a tough act to follow after the war and couldn't find it. Brando was their other hero. When his biker character in *The Wild Ones* was asked, "What are you rebelling against?" he answered, "What have you got?"

As an actor, I am aware of an irony now that I never considered until I began this book. If Dean had lived, he would have not been mourned as a lost idol but appreciated as a movie star. I wonder if he would have been smart enough to recognize the need for a sequel that brought his character to his own fatherhood; would he have made the mistakes his generation made, or could he have seen with some wisdom what could not have been seen then?

Dean died, and *Rebel* would never be looked at for its content. That content is the story I'm telling you now.

His generation was born too late to help fight World War II, but they were too old to march or take acid with the boomers. They had studied Civics as well as it could be taught during the war, but they were also the first TV generation, and could see both Disney's idealized America as well as the Civil Rights marches attacked by law enforcement and the Klan, especially in the South, where they were often the same. They were trapped between the tales of heroism of their fathers, the never-discussed subject, and the diminished man, angst-ridden for a raise, who wearily came home every night, never talking about the war or much else, only sitting in front of the television news without comment until dinner. This was a puzzle, a mystery. Was this the same man who had a hidden pile of military medals the son had found by accident?

But the aftermath of the war wasn't easy even for the victors. The willingness to go to war is easy, the willingness to aim for wisdom and restrain the warrior far, far harder. And that lack of wisdom extended to Mom; she was not the same woman he left behind for the war. She had her name changed. No longer Mom. No longer Betty or Helen. She was Rosie,

Rosie the Riveter. During wartime, she kept America together, kept the American economy going. She also kept her family going. She kept women going. She got the first dose of self-esteem that women had had in centuries. She kept waiting for the other shoe to drop, finding out she was a widow.

I don't think there's another group of people anywhere any time who'd been so overwhelmed with conflicting thoughts than American women when the Big Lunk came home from the war. She loved him. I hope he kissed Mom and took her to bed for a week. When they came out again, I hope he said "thank you" for taking up the slack as Rosie the Riveter—*that was sweet, pumpkin*—because right after that he unknowingly took away from her a solid portion of her self-worth. *That's Dad's job now.*

Rosie was going to be too busy booming out babies in bunches. There was no one she could turn to for help in unweaving the feelings of gratitude, rage, resentment, bewilderment, anger, love—love of freedom and love of being directly responsible for an important part of the war effort, then being discarded without a thought. She lay next to him with such a cluster of conflicting thoughts and feelings. Unquestionably she loved him, had missed him, had sustained him and been sustained by him. She had this fierce desire to smash a frying pan into his happy snoring face. The only thing to do was what people have always done in the face of unavoidable mixed messages. It's what the gals on the prairies did when they found themselves alone for another winter without husband, with six children all wailing, on farms where the neighbors were ten miles down the road, with snow drifting in to imprison them for months, isolated women trying to think over the children wailing again and again. . . . Either take a jug of "Mother's Little Helper" as sold by the traveling snake oil salesman or take an ax to the children and enter them into the books as "Victims of Prairie Fever."

Prairie fever was alive and well as Rosie watched her guy, the Big Lunk, take her job from her, with no one wise enough to think of it as a problem to be solved, so after the war Mother's Little Helper was morphed into Librium and a generation of American women got loaded to put some sparkle into the suburbs. A slurred sparkle, as it were—another mixed message. Nor did she have the wisdom to forgive her suburban children when they took drugs a decade or so later.

The new technology of television was not seen or felt as addiction. It was all a splendid pleasure; everyone got something special, from those wanting to laugh with Phil Silvers or Jackie Gleason, or hum along with Dinah Shore, to the ones who wanted to think with *Omnibus* or *College Bowl*, or absorb great theater like *Playhouse 90*. Television offered up Sid Caesar, Steve Allen, and Jack Parr as well as Walter Cronkite and Edward R. Murrow. Bernstein's "Concerts in the Park for Children" were not only for children.

TV also taught us about sex, though not necessarily human. It covered all life from water buffalos to lions, to polar bears and cheetahs, all those documentaries earning surprising popularity because they were about the "Two Fs": Fighting and Fucking.

(Do hyenas consider David Attenborough a pornographer? As a human mammal I confess to changing the channel often, because monkey sex doesn't do it for me. What is the science that explains the visual power of showing procreation mechanics to cause in humans such a strange mix of reactions? Do house pets wait with infinite patience for their human masters to leave the house before they rush to their TVs or *Animal Life* magazines?)

Americans were delighted with the sense of instantaneous knowledge, worlds of human endeavor that expanded their minds, and introduced an astonishment at how amazing life on this planet could be. And entertainment for free, or at least for the cost of an electronic appliance. Parents thought it great that they could plunk their children in front of the TV without even a babysitter. And televisions looked good as a piece of furniture in their living rooms. It was only after they turned it on that it turned into a hypnotic.

Television didn't heal what lay beneath the Deaners. They were in an evolutionary struggle that went back millions of years, the struggle for survival itself. It was visible (or very soon to be) on television documentaries about life on this planet, which sooner or later gets to killing for a meal: jaguars taking down antelope, and young jaguars, like young antelope, spoiling for an intergenerational fight. We, being mammals too, were right in the middle of our version. For the children of the Greatest Generation it was particularly hard, because their fathers' generational heroism was part of public record, known to all including the sons, so finding a way to compete, however unconscious, was almost impossible.

Could these fathers, many now middle-management types preoccupied with material success, be the same men found in hidden pictures, next to hidden medals, next to hidden papers that translated their hospital release, unmistakable proof of Dad as that grinning hotshot in groups of other hotshots, dealing with real battles and real wounds? Did their children know that many of them lived in housing America gave them as a gift, a grateful thank-you for what was unspeakably awful? Was that the real reason for never talking about it? Or the diploma that made Dad

a lawyer—that too was a gift? How do you talk about
horror and fear? And why would you want to relive all
that? The fathers had no understanding of the consequences of their silence. That silence was a learned
thing and passed from generation to generation.

As adults the Deaners watched reporters arrested
live on TV during the Democratic convention of 1968.
They saw the mayor of Chicago yelling "Fuck you" at
the reporters. They watched as young people wearing
outlandish clothing got beaten by Chicago cops.

They watched the breakdown of their own society,
bloody, surprising, an unmitigated defeat to political activism. It frightened them more than the Battle
of the Bulge. Television had become a Pandora's box.
The norms of civic education didn't stand a chance
against the nightly news, and the lessons taught as a
strong defense against political breakdown were swept
away by images of 1968. Out of their wits, discordant,
the James Dean Generation reacted to the perceived
anarchy as incorrectly as they could. By the 1970s,
they were in public office, on school boards. They
looked back with horror at the '60s. What the protes-
tors saw as an exercise of their rights as Americans,
the Deaners saw as anarchy, blood in the streets, the
result of too much emphasis on activism.

The James Deaners had married and had kids, and
looking back over their shoulders and watching their
sleeping children, they felt a terror that it would
be their own young who were beaten, that becoming
active citizens could get them killed. That was reason enough to remove from their consciousness their
ties to the creation of the most important political
invention in the history of human civilization.

So, for our own good . . . they sought to de-
emphasize participatory citizenship.

They thought that exiling the American Revolution

up one flight and down the hall to social studies would do the job, turning the freedoms achieved at such a bloody cost and the ideas behind them into a gentle overview of "Our Way of Life," a panorama of cities and farmlands from sea to shining sea.

When we moved Civics to social studies, its context was narrowed. We didn't compare what we created with what the world once was, nor the reason it was called a Revolution. When we put our governance structure, and the values we espoused, in the context of world history, only then can we see what we had created. We had created the most important political revolution in the history of civilization.

By hiding the actual facts from our history and civics lessons, they were utterly changing the meaning of these events, taking the pride of our enormous accomplishment and wadding it up and tossing it. Our pearl beyond price, which required all of human history to produce, the largest step ever in moral progress, was sidelined when measured against what they saw on TV. Silence again, like an inherited disease . . .

They reduced us all to indifferent readers of history, not makers of it. No more We the People changing the world.

The James Dean Generation, in their determination to do what they thought was best, ignored that they were attacking the central mythology of America and diluting the justification for calling us any kind of revolutionary anything. They were diluting the ties of respect for the concepts of freedom of thought and due process of law, breaking the deal that made sense of our radical doctrines, and breaking the promise to teach our values to each separate generation.

Civics education began disappearing by the mid-seventies and was almost gone by the middle of Reagan's presidency. How many hundreds of thousands of students have passed through our education system since then? More critically, how many office holders went through their school years with as little knowledge about government as their classmates? How many people of the Left and Right graduated from high school with a stunted understanding of governance and never thought about entering politics until years later, when a specific issue got them so riled up that it moved them to consider running for office? Americans in their forties, with little or no higher education, emotionally linked to one issue with no immersion in the concepts that created America as so different from other countries? With all of Reagan's wonderful talk about America's greatness—and the talk *was* wonderful—we had never been as far away from the ideas that the world called American as we were by the end of Reagan's term in office.

Reagan embodied conservativism while he was president. Now there are people who call themselves conservatives and consider Reagan wishy-washy. After Reagan, both parties were increasingly defined by the extreme ends of each. Moderate Republicans and centrist Democrats are defined as "cowardly," and not enough people see the harm, while Tea Party types and far-left newcomers criticize those with some experience in getting things done, in working with the other party as they are intended to. Is it acceptable to America now that so many will give credence to only one political party? Is it really sensible to think that all opinions that differ from yours are subversive? Do we really think that all good Americans must agree with one another, and if you don't you're an enemy of all that is good?

The time from 1965 to today is like the distance from here to Mars.

Chapter 10

A Crumbling Foundation

Iappeared on the Tucker Carlson show saying much of what you've just read, including that Civics hasn't been taught in American schools since the 1970s. A number of people wrote in saying, "Dreyfuss. You're nuts. I took Civics in 1986" or "1993." They are misinterpreting what's changed and misunderstanding what's been lost. I am speaking about losing clarity on what Civics was meant to be and how it was originally taught.

To clarify, Civics was never a subject meant to be taught only in one year or one semester. It was introduced to students in a given year, usually fourth grade. It was called History in that semester, called Government in others, and all the while as part of American History from the colonial period to the War of Independence to the inauguration of the first president, George Washington.

There have never been classes called "Clarity of Thought" or "Agility of Mind 101." These are civic tools, practiced and honed by good teachers in constant connection with their students in a kind of "Socratic dialogue" in all classes from English Lit to Geography to Home Economics. These tools meant that the interactions between teachers and students were civil, inquiring, and intended to provoke debate and curiosity. It meant that art, for instance, could inform science and vice versa. It meant that all classes were connectable. Civic discourse, the respect for opposing views, and the talents to work together were prized because Civics gave procedures and rules and intellectual allowance.

Today this is not so. We have eviscerated the education of the young. We have cut their classes down to a utilitarian sparseness and denied them resources. We have reduced our respect for their teachers, viewing them as sly, defensive cheaters, instead of the few remaining heroes of our culture. And teachers are the ones you can thank for saving many, many parents from serving long prison terms for manslaughter, and you know what I'm talking about.

We deprive students of the large territory that public schools used to fill. Do they learn music and perform in orchestras? Do they have theater departments for performing and learning the cultural importance of Shakespeare? Do they take shop, and take apart and put together a fifteen-year-old laptop computer, and learn self-reliance and teamwork? Do they take English Literature and learn the imperialist poetry of Kipling and the anti-imperialist writing of Mark Twain? Tell me that they learn a history of America that includes, but isn't dominated by, the mistakes we've made, the struggle that all immigrants went through, and the record-breaking list of broken promises our government has with our Native population.

Do our children experience any learning that will be of central import within a few months or years of their graduation?

Public school years are not the years of expertise, of straight-A work across the board. It's the time for the foundations to be laid. It's the time when certain civic tools needed in any or all endeavors are drilled into our youngest, so that later, after they decide to be scientists, airline pilots, or barbers, they have a strong foundation to build their expertise on. It's not necessary to understand how the economy runs in any great detail, but to use those years to acquire the basics.

Is home economics where they learn how to build a family budget, or is it also the introduction to our kids' understanding of things that they will need in the real world, with real money? Will they understand mortgages or bank loans, and will they have any connection with "the financial industry" that might help them navigate their real lives? Home Ec should answer critical questions: What is a bank? What is a credit union? What's the difference? What's the prime rate? What's the Fed? Who prints the money? Who owns the Fed? What's the real difference between buying a car on credit and buying the whole thing in one lump sum? Is it true that you pay ten times more when you pay on credit? Is debt good or bad? What is bankruptcy? Do our children learn how to run a business endeavor? Do they learn enough to understand the competition that is out to make them unemployed?

Are they given a history of any issue, as in why we have the foreign policy interests we have, or why race is still a problem? Are they taught to think

clearly enough that they won't just accept the opinions of commentators who speak without expertise to
listeners who are not equipped to know the difference
between what is and what is not?

When they graduate, *are they as smart as they have
a right to be*? And if not, *why not*?

Today's education system is the consequence of at
least fifty years of irresponsible civic behavior by
almost everyone who drank the Kool-Aid and dropped
stunned into toxically bad citizenship. Our present
stewards of society apparently give no thought to how
usefully bright and intellectually sensible students
should be as they turn out of high school. So short-
sighted and angst-ridden for all the wrong reasons.
As if worrying about "whether or not kids in school
are getting the best education because they are going
to damn well need it" just doesn't rise to the level
of the anxiety that "it's costing too much, we are
barely staying above the poverty line and you want to
have higher taxes? Are you out of your mind!?"

No, I'm NOT.

Someone must say aloud what no one wants to hear.
Taxes are not the rewards of pickpockets. Taxes are
the only meaningful gesture of sharing the responsibilities of the caretaking of America. They are the
way cops and firemen and public school teachers get
paid. We should all grow up and stop whining like
little kids. You might disagree with some of what we
pay for with taxes, but the reason and logic of taxes
is indisputable. I suggest each of you do the exercise of writing out your version of what you think
taxes should pay for. Try it. It won't kill you. Compare with your friends; compare with those you think
are not friends. Try it.

I think you're going to find that people with lots
of money end the exercise still having lots of money.

Many don't pay enough and many are proud of it. Look how proud Trump expected us all to be as he described how good he was at denying his due to the country. I know we all try to do that in some form, but do we consider the consequences if all of us succeed in paying less?

The real answer to "how much of our budget should public school cost?" should be **"Whatever it takes."** But the realists on school boards would be open-jawed with astonishment whenever they heard that answer.

Those who do not know the nation's birth tale and its unique demands have deprived the public schools; thus, the slide into educational decay began, to be quietly followed by a general decay in our society, until we bumped into today.

We are the richest country in the history of man's imagination, and **we can't afford to educate our children?** Or for that matter fix our bridges, dams, and potholes, or plan for disasters. . . . Do we have any idea how neurotic we are? How the world is holding its breath, taking odds on when we collapse completely?

The James Deaners allowed the holes in our historic birth tale, and its story of the most dramatic change in governance was blandly overlooked. Those holes became filled with anxiety and panic, and when education was subject to cost analysis, school budgets became a casualty.

Given time, the James Deaners might have discovered their error themselves, but before that could happen, the scent of profit had put dreams into the brains of Profiteers. They are the ones who made certain that they confused the educators and the parents enough that they kept trying to make the right to private profit a right that shouldn't be denied and one superior to the right to a comprehensive education.

Private profit is fatal to quality education. The

good reputation of most if not all private or charter schools is due in some small part to underpaying
teachers; the irony of that is the implication that
teachers in public schools are overpaid, which is a
punchline in a Stephen Colbert monologue.

"Privatizing" education is serious business, but
a business. Private and charter schools are as deep
into dishonesty as Bernie Madoff was. "Charter" is a
code for racial exclusivity, also known as "segregation." It's leaving the Black and Latino and immigrant
groups to the underfunded public schools, while the
privileged fill charter schools and private schools,
even while paying the same taxes that support public
schools.

Some statistics say, after vigorous editing, that
charters deliver quality education. Some might, if
they are worked with the dedication and inspiration
of a few, but in general they work no better than
normal public schools. You can find the same amount
of historical inaccuracy, and drug taking, gangs,
bullying, jot for jot, as in public schools. I have
kids who went to private, and whose friends went to
public. My kids and their friends brought home the
same texts whether from public or private. The only
difference was that fewer boys in the private schools
wore swastikas tattooed on their styled bald heads.

What if we as a country decided that our kids'
education was meant to be first priority, not last,
if we were good enough to commit ourselves to making all public schools as wide and deep as we can
afford, so that every high school district could be
Beverly Hills School District? It could be, if we had
the courage and wisdom.

To destroy our faith in public schools, the priva-
teers bring up all the usual suspects to create sus-
picion against public institutions: More and Bigger

Government, sly teachers, violence in public schools. It's as if someone is trying to define as fundamental and obvious and un-American, the Big Government, with dictatorial power and bureaucratic inefficiency. Americans can feel that way because the Constitution and the Bill of Rights haven't been taught as central to their or their children's education.

We live in a system in American society that requires the active involvement of the people. That is, unless we are opting for a mediocre education that, compared with that of my generation, is an eviscerated and empty vessel. Fifty years is past the limit. It would be impossible to claim pride of invention, how in history our comparison to all other regimes before us was so liberating it could only be compared to an opium dream.

If you don't teach our values in schools, what are you teaching them? That they are not as bright as those earlier generations? Or that we don't care if they learn anything as long as they pass from grade to grade?

If I were pitching a film to a studio with a story about all of this, I would make the villains the ones who are seeing big profit in privatizing the school system and taking down the public school system altogether. The only ones who have a dog in this hunt are those profiteers. In the pitch I would say, "Hey, I know—we'll make the major villain a billionaire woman who is secretary of education and who is arrogant enough to let people know she'd like to give private profit a turn and take down this rickety public system. And we'll call her Betsy." I'm calling her Betsy DeVos, who was a disgrace as secretary of education. It's like the Coyote buying the Acme Company. Except it's not funny.

Charter schools are the path to a native aristocracy

. . . and they reek of dishonesty as a new source
of private profit. Profit is the most powerful toxic
plague; especially in education, it has taken down
honesty, accountability, and integrity, and created
more denial than can be good for anyone.

Chapter 11

Unfair Capitalism

Now, let me clarify where I stand on something, because it is too easy to let senselessness topple logic when financial matters come into the discussion.

1776 could be called a "magic number," because that was the year that two documents appeared that changed the world. The Declaration of Independence appealed to the masses through the prose of Thomas Jefferson. In addition, Adam Smith published *The Wealth of Nations*. Smith, a friend of Ben Franklin, was possibly the greatest economist since the Big Bang; in fact, he virtually created the study of the economy. In his book, he describes in detail a specific process that was central to the nations of the world, but thus far had not been understood by anyone who was deeply involved in it already.

- A lady in London wants to buy a fur hat.
- A French Canadian trapper catches certain animals whose fur is prized.
- A button maker in Marseille makes buttons, clasps, and all sorts of devices in varying designs.

Adam Smith connected the dots of all these people who were firmly associated in an endeavor without understanding the whole, each of them getting a benefit in cooperation with the others. Smith described the process in detail and called it "capitalism."

The Wealth of Nations quickly became the bible of capitalism, yet probably went unread by most capitalists. Smith declared firmly that Labor cannot make a product without Capital and as firmly declared that Capital cannot make a product without Labor; therefore, Capital and Labor were perfect partners. Both deserved to sit as equals at the same table. Smith also laid down some rules of this partnership: There must be a minimum wage set (!), and Labor must be allowed to have unions, since "Capital has already unionized" (!!). Significantly, Capital must be closely scrutinized because left to themselves Capitalists will behave like predatory beasts (!!!).

I believe that capitalism and republican democracy are potentially perfect partners, allowing for creativity toward social as well as commercial purposes, so long as capital does not achieve unfair advantage. If the individuals who control capital operate under the same rules, being subject to the same legally applied punishments as those in all classes, then we might have a shot at an indescribably grand life. Unfortunately, we have never lived with a fairly applied system that has not been perverted by capital's advantages, seen or unseen. Capitalism could be fair or fairer, but trying to tell us that it has been fair in this country is a sick, patronizing joke.

When I played Bernie Madoff, the biggest crook on Wall Street, I learned his answer to any and all who asked him how he did it: "My gut." "My gut" was the only answer he ever gave. His gut caused hundreds of otherwise intelligent people to hand him all their money, all they had earned and saved and made, until they had given him billions. What's funny is that if you were shopping for people who might help your money make money, considered straight shooters untainted by criminal behavior, they would all flourish colorful pie charts and repeat arcane, incomprehensible paragraphs memorized at the Wharton School, ending the sell with something very similar to "My gut."

There were many companies who worked with Madoff, yet because he was caught and confessed and they didn't, they are not guilty, even though they knew of all along, and abetted, his criminal activity. He depended on them to make his scheme workable. Quietly. One or two of them actually closed their businesses in anticipation of having to answer to authorities, so they just stopped, waiting for the ax to fall, which it didn't, because the finance system counts on people being dumb as ducks.

What did Madoff do to cover his actions? Ahh, brilliant. He opened a savings account in the bank next door, deposited billions of dollars into a single account, and drew from the account whatever was necessary when a client wanted to end his fiduciary relationship with his trusted friend Bernie. Now, if you owned a bank that had the usual kind of accounts, except for one which had billions accruing interest at a normal rate for a savings and loan, ya think that bank knew he was doing something odd and illegal?

You betcha.

After Justice Sandra Day O'Connor retired from the US Supreme Court, she created iCivics, a program that was both a study of the Constitution and a work program where students got the chance to do some version of real-world practical political work. At one point, we had a meeting to see if I would be interested in getting involved and partnering with her iCivics program. In the end, I decided Justice O'Connor and I would not be a good fit, coincidentally the exact conclusion she was coming to about partnering with me. During our meeting I asked her a question.

"How could you let money be the entry to a political career?"

"What's wrong with money?" she said.

I replied, "Well, if it's the only value, and it is, there's lots wrong with it. It's the reason why we left the British Empire to begin with, and it makes it impossible for a citizen who is not wealthy to enter politics without making alliances with wealth. They could not compete with those who can afford TV advertising time."

She said, "You're wrong."

And that's all she said.

In 1816 Thomas Jefferson said, "I hope we shall crush in its birth the aristocracy of our monied corporations which dare already to challenge our government to a trial of strength, and bid defiance to the laws of our country."

Our courts, led by the Supreme Court, allow for criminally unbalanced concepts, like the equal standing of corporations as humans in the eyes of the law. This is an absurdity of senselessness, where profit subverts reason. It is unfair because the rule makers in corporations can hide when those rules cause death or damage; they are not criminally accountable, due to the "corporation" being the only one punishable, and only by monetary fines. Make that offer to murderers or child molesters, why don't we?

Legal historians have pointed out that the Supreme Court decision from the 1880s that declared corporations to have the same legal status as human persons is built on a fiction. A fake.

It's a fake. It never happened.

Mountains of law have been deposited on top of this pile of filth, and all of it pro-business and anti-labor. I'm about to say something that no author should say, but put my book down now and go read UCLA professor Adam Winkler's book, *We the Corporations*. It tells the whole story and it's one you really must hear. I, despite a talent for cursing, am stumped for words by that story. I just can't describe the nausea I felt when I read it.

Anyone who says we really have a fairly applied legal code that guarantees liberty and justice for all is either brainwashed, brain-dead, or evil. I respect the written Constitution's insistence that it be central. I have little respect for the senselessness of spinning legal fantasies out of either liberal or conservative activism on the court. When a liberal court sought to amend educational segregation by ordering busing, *it ignored the pace that citizens were willing to move and overstepped the possible*. Or when the conservative court began the same "Gotcha!" game by telling women they had no right to make the decisions that only the individual woman could sensibly make.

Or take your interfering courts back to reality, and stop imposing Baptist or Catholic creed onto all. For that matter, stop imposing Liberal Creed or Conservative Creed onto all.

That especially applies to the highest court in

the land. Personally, I think the current fad of "originalism" expressed by the conservative majority on the present Supreme Court is laughable criminal bunk. Excuse me? We are to interpret the words of the Constitution as they were understood at the time of its writing? None of the founders were linguistic experts. Nor did they have authority to decree the singular definition of a word. I can point you to three different definitions used at that time for the word "militia." And one of them was the arming of slave owners. Was that in some original justices' minds? How could we know? Originalism could be a smokescreen for any particularly unpleasant interpretation, since it really can't be exactly defined.

Justice Scalia's arguments that ended controls over guns take the comedy prize for illogic and inconsistency of thought. Did Scalia's reading of the Second Amendment advance any cause other than taking the Court away from its responsibilities? Don't make me laugh. I'm an American, so perhaps I'm too intellectually infirm to follow his Rube Goldberg reasoning.

I would say the same for the sometimes liberal belief in equality of outcome so that all are assured of success in life; everyone on the team gets a prize, so no one has hurt feelings. It is a tragic misperception of the human character, and the idea of reparations for the crimes of our ancestors is an equal misreading of the concept of responsibility, since politics is the Art of the Possible. I condemn both parties for bending the Constitution to push their agendas over the long-term health of the country. The Constitution should be there day and night, storm or clear skies. That is not to be confused with political parties bending in the wind. Wherever shame is being hidden, gagged and bound, sooner or later it will return and scorch the courts for dismantling gun control, or for busing and other forms of social tinkering, for hurrying the pace toward someone's idea of a higher morality and instead causing chaos, anger, and fear.

The Supreme Court is rarely made up of professors who know the law. Instead, the Supreme Court is the supreme reward for party service, and always has been. That has become more and more clear in our age of senselessness. Trump's court is McConnell's reward for service to the GOP, and is consistent with the GOP, not the Constitution. At one time, decades ago, it was FDR's court.

Today's Supreme Court is now considered the most conservative in history since before FDR's time. It was the Court that passed *Citizens United*, essentially making money the prime mover of our political system. It provides the most brazen attempt to kill the exercise of freedom by denying people without wealth—or unwilling to suck up to wealth—to choose a political career.

By removing all caps on money donated to politics, and by making a career in politics impossible for anyone but the wealthy or those who appeal to them, and by allowing the money donated to be anonymous, which part of the virtues and values of America are not being trashed? Thank you, John Roberts, for showing the world that, when given the chance to rise above party and achieve judicial greatness by serving all the American people, you choose not to.

Some of us might be smart enough to recognize *Citizens United* as the most disgraceful decision ever, but the Supreme Court was clearly assuming otherwise. They assume we aren't able to tie our shoes. Thank you, John Roberts, and send my regards to the late Justice Lewis Powell Jr. for his fifty-four-page memo describing how to drag the law back to the era before the Civil War, when corruption haunted our young democracy. Jane Mayer, in her book *Dark Money*, explains all this far better than I can, and it should be required reading, before our kids are denied the ability to read by the next generation of justices who decide that public education is not cost-effective.

We are now as weightless and free of accountability as can be.

Jeff Bezos, the richest man in the country, was fined $62 million for cheating his employees out of their tips. He certainly didn't have to because he's one of the richest men in the world. He did it because he could. He exempts himself from any social responsibility. As he told Boris Johnson, the former PM of Great Britain, "It's your job to make Amazon pay more taxes." Speechless, I am.

There's no doubt our decay has been helped along by America's oldest adversary, the monied interests who watched us become victims of a plague of their making, that destroys all virtues and makes one vice appear as virtue to the exclusion of all else: Profit. That right to profit, not included in the Bill of Rights for good reason, has taken down honesty and accountability. Those interests have acted with a talent for patience that waits with careful calibration for the moment they can trust that few will be outraged, that the idea of the participating citizen is dulled and gone, and then they step in to seize their rewards.

We are becoming the worst enemy of our Founders: a society divided between the powerful, wealthy few and the overruled majority. This is true even in something as basic to a civilized society as healthcare. Some doctors now sell "concierge medicine" to extract profit from patients, departing from the historic

definition of doctoring by breaking the Hippocratic
Oath on a daily basis. Where I live near San Diego
I find business cards in doctors' offices describing
"concierge medicine" as "pay more, get better service," such as house calls, no waiting, twenty-four-
hour availability—things that were traditionally a
part of all doctors' practices. Doctors deserve com-
pensation; I don't argue that point at all. But must
it come by creating a division between rich patients
and poor patients?

In the way of things, the urge for wealth, more
money, and the practice of unfair capitalism corrodes
any institution it comes in contact with. No sector
of our society is immune.

Chapter 12

A Word from de Tocqueville

*America is the only country in the history of the world
that is bound only by ideas. They have no common
religion, no common caste or class; they are devoted to
no bloodline, or to any ancestral achievement. They
are bound only by the ideas of the enlightenment, and
if these ideas are not taught to every separate generation, they are not bound.*

—ALEXIS DE TOCQUEVILLE, *DEMOCRACY IN AMERICA* (1837)

It is 2022. I submit we are now not so bound.

Chapter 13

Technology Overload

Technology has been changing the world ever since the dawn of invention. The wheel advanced every empire, and if there was an empire that didn't adopt it, the empire disappeared. When a new technology arrives, it forces a transformation in fundamentals like distance and time and one's way of life. I can see the calligraphers who composed the parchments at the end of the Middle Ages meeting at the nearest tavern, getting pie-eyed and muttering against the demon printing press.

Once a technology appears, it evolves. At first, when Alexander Bell invented the telephone, the tech was in its unsatisfactory infancy. Even as it developed, people had to get used to it. So lawyer Smith and wife would scream into the phone because the human brain couldn't accept that you needn't scream yourself hoarse to be heard on the other end across town. Over the decades telephone technology changed.

Users learned to talk in a normal tone. Our brains had 150 years of practice teaching us to deal with party lines and long-distance operators. Everything was settled until Steve Jobs came along and blew things up.

The first smartphones were simple slabs, like bricks, built at first without a set of instructions such as "no need to yell." But brains hadn't adjusted, and people yelled even though the phone was barely two inches above the lips. If Jobs had designed the iPhone with an angled bottom of 3 percent or 5 percent, maybe the brain would be confident that the angle permitted even whispering. Maybe we all would have conversed in normal tones and there would have been no fistfights at Starbucks or road rage, when one driver made insane by another driver's inability to drive and talk on a cell phone causes them to pull out a gun and start shooting. Steve Jobs and his little band of merry men knew a lot more about electronics than ergonomics.

Our media tech spread all over the world, so people in Nigeria or Cairo could see the Towers fall at the exact instant as people in Kansas. We have instantaneous information (and misinformation) and instantaneous reactions, which demand instantaneous and reflexive responses. Horror, hatred, outrage—the emotions felt at the moment—become the only emotions. They don't give way to rumination or clarity. The air is filled with the same terrible clips, the same blaring intro music, the same screaming fonts, the same clips again, the same screaming fonts, again and again. There's no time to reflect, to inquire. Even the mere suggestion of such a thing as thinking things through is suspect, even unpatriotic. All that's required is to nod our heads while we grieve, rage, and react.

After the World Trade Center fell, it was proof
of God's sense of humor that the first thing Americans demanded was a sovereign who could act on his
own. They had faith that the leaders knew who did it,
where they were, and how to get them—not just in one
foreign nation, but in others. They attacked anyone
who questioned the Commander in Chief, or changed
their minds when new facts were revealed. Changing
your mind implies new information factored into decision making. If your leaders are saying that thoughtful reflection based on newly revealed facts is for
sissies, then you can be labeled as "flip-flopping"
and demonized for changing your mind.

Our ability to deny that we are in an Ocean of
Denial has made all our problems more difficult than
they might have been. We would not have had to pretend about all these errors and refusals that add up
to pretending about Being America. Worse, we would
not have become addicted to playing pretend.

But people are, however, people; meaning that people, unlike, say . . . jaguars . . . do not always
operate at peak efficiency. Jaguars hunt the hunt-
able. Jaguars don't laze about while the river dries
up, just because it is a sunny day.

And people as individuals are not always wise. Many
people refuse to say "I don't know," or "I changed my
mind."

That's known in other quarters as "learning."

In an era when our electronic media supply us with
instant access to more information than ever, we
have not paid attention to the new rules. Not enough
attention has been paid to the different ways society
has bent and twisted itself into shapes around this
magical but complex thing, or the ways this technology can be used against us. New processes require new
thinking. As these technologies become more central

to our lives, we refuse to acknowledge that they might need serious study, or might include possible dangers that function in surreptitious ways.

We all know this at some level. We have known this for a long time but have done nothing to change the direction in which we are headed.

We are infatuated with our technology. That explains how Steve, Jeff, Elon, and the entire nation of South Korea could become so rich. But that still leaves us with an enormous ignorance of how these things have changed us, made us less in some ways, altering our sense of public and private, making us react unthinkingly to things that we should slow down to understand.

Is it true that our children have a diminishing ability to concentrate? Or that we are condemned to listen in Starbucks to the personal conversations of others, conducted in a loud voice? Or that going to a movie includes the challenge of trying to ignore people talking back to the screen, forgetting they're not at home? Don't we all need to step back to see if the weave and design of our lives needs attending? Shouldn't we take a look at the atmosphere of our society, heated up enough by tech so that we are less patient than we should be, more eager to believe what's not true and to respond unthinkingly, and more angry and divided as Americans?

I identify cable channels that call themselves "news channels" as "affirmative news channels" because what you get from them is mainly affirmation of your political biases. Fox, MSNBC, CNN, and the like are opinion spreaders, and they lack the constitutionally endorsed idea of opposing views. If they were simply called "opinion channels," I'd have no objection. I admit to being intensely curious about who would.

When I spoke to the National Press Club a few years ago, I asked, "Have you seen George Clooney's movie *Good Night, and Good Luck*? Most likely you have, because it's all about you. Did it make you uneasy? Did it keep you up that night? Did you think Edward R. Murrow was talking to someone else when he said, 'If news is to be regarded as a commodity, only acceptable when saleable, then I don't care what you call it—I say it isn't news.'

"Murrow foretold the future, which is our present. You are the stewards of that particular slice of America. I am tempted to ask, 'Will those of you who consider yourselves the heirs of Edward Murrow please raise your hands,' but I won't. I wouldn't want to start a fight or threaten my sense of humor. But I will say that if American television news people believe that the news does its job and fulfills its mandate, that it does the right thing in its obligations to this country, I am sorrier than I can express.

"I have lived long enough to remember a smarter America, with a truly free press, and it was *Meet the Press* with a locked door. A politician took the risk of being trapped on camera, unable to escape the press doing its rude job for us, asking a question for the fourth time. It meant that affirmative news didn't exist; you had to watch network TV news, which jumbled together the stuff you liked and hated into the same broadcast. It meant retaining the mature ability of hearing news you didn't like. It meant conservative Democrats and liberal Republicans, and civilized discourse, and temperament and decency expected as part of leadership. It meant knowing that America had to be run by educated adults, with policies fact-checked by educated adults."

What happened to these bright, thoughtful members of the press that made them forget the spirit of America they knew in their bones they were betraying?

They certainly have forgotten other critical things, like the need for a Fairness Doctrine. Cable networks are completely free of any such thing. We thought we needed a Fairness Doctrine when we only had three networks. And then, with the rise of cable and the internet, of course Presidents Reagan, the Bushes, and Obama decided this was the issue to come together on, and all agreed to kill any government insistence on fairness and government control over what we laughingly call the news networks.

We have a notion of what this doctrine is and we get it from "Fairness." We don't do it as well as we think we did. We've closed the door on fairness and gone the other way. What's wrong with contining to strive for fairness?

It used to be that the government was supposed to protect us from obvious bullshit in television, in the financial markets, in educational institutions that were supposed to be teaching the values underlying the Constitution. Today we see government interference as our enemy. The real enemy is the government not interfering. Any comments, Mr. President?

I once had the honor of addressing a group of judges, many of them chief justices of the various states, in Anchorage around 2011. At that time I was ignorant of the fact that the Fairness Doctrine was no longer in place and that it hadn't been since Reagan's administration. I was not only ignorant of that, but ignorant of the fact that both President George W. Bush and President Barack Obama wanted to redo the Fairness Doctrine, but neither of them did in the slightest way. I did not specifically mention the Fairness Doctrine in my speech, so I just lucked out by chance from being perceived as an idiot.

I told the group of judges, "I'm going to ask you all a question, but first I am going to say that I am not a lawyer, although in my family I am surrounded by them; throw a rock in any direction at any family gathering and you'll hit an attorney, so I have lived within the atmosphere of the Law. Now, the question: You receive a letter from your local television news outlet, stating that from then on traffic news will require a $4.00 surcharge. How do you respond?"

Everyone in the banquet hall shook their heads "no."

"Because that's their job, right?"

Heads nodded "yes."

"Because they are obligated, correct?"

"Yes."

"Which is why the networks were not owned by those who ran them, but they were licensed, yes?"

"Yes" by all the judges in attendance.

"Known or not to the public at large, network television started out as owned by the people of the nation, and the networks had to fulfill their obligations to us before they were entitled to profit from the arrangement."

I continued, "So that they promised to cover the news without interference or bias, or change the presentation of news to fit a particular political point of view, or favor one kind of soap or another. Right?"

Right.

"Especially because politics is not a product, subject to market rules, nor are they entitled to profit from its coverage, right?"

Right.

"And yet that's exactly what is happening today."

Networks design the presentation of political news, and in recent memory they allowed the political parties to fire the League of Women Voters, who used to run the televised political debates and were strict in their evenhandedness. Now the party in the White House manages the debates and sets new rules for what is asked and by whom, and the networks reap the profits from the product called the news as if it were soap or cereal.

Is there anyone who would argue with the description that the debates in 2016 or 2020 were closer to vaudeville than politics? All they lacked were red noses and clown feet, the big floppy kind. And can anyone say that the press was functioning as the thoughtful outsider with the power to represent you and me, by being the adults we needed them to be? The blatant pettiness and kindergarten behavior of the brats running for the presidency could have been stopped, a timeout given to all, if the press were doing its real job.

Imagine the response that could have been from any one of the members of the press who covered the debates:

"I have been sitting here astonished and appalled with one thought in my head: What would Ed Murrow have done in this situation? Would he permit this childishness? For how long? I'm not Ed Murrow, but I can aspire to be like him because he really was the best of us. I withdraw from this so-called debate and hope all participating will follow my example. We must rethink all this, because it is an immediate danger to democracy. I realize I have been worrying about losing my job rather than doing my job. What I see is no one large enough to be presidential. Quite the opposite. Therefore, I am leaving my post as of this minute."

That is what should have been said . . . if only.

There is a direct line between the extraordinarily high advertising fees now charged by television and all other costs of political campaigns. It is why we now speak of campaigns costing billions of dollars. Nearly all that money goes to television, and all that money has distorted our political system. I believe that if you want to run a political campaign, you can spend the money on billboards, in magazines, on special presentations on the internet—on radio, even, but not television.

As I told the judges, I would risk little by betting that most or all of you here today know there is a certain wrongness in this. Politics is not a product. It should not be for sale to the highest bidder. Period.

I have grown impatient with talk of campaign finance reform. If we have accepted how much is charged for showing debates or how much the rules are twisted for guiding them, the pact has already been signed with the devil. And I want some protection that's comprehensive and powerful enough to put my America beyond the reach of Lucifer and his human minions.

I want an amendment to the Constitution that creates unbreakable firewalls between money, television, and politics. If the government cannot restrict free speech, the parties and the profiteers should not be able to gag the press and prevent it from asking important questions, or reduce the time given for complex answers, thus refusing to fulfill the notion of an informed citizenry. All of this is being done, right now, by the partnership of parties and television "news."

Many other countries are firmer in their control over the electronic media. Yes, our Constitution

protects the freedom of speech, but—again—the Constitution is not a suicide pact. Money has destroyed
our political system, aided by distorted rulings from
the Supreme Court like *Citizens United*, and we look
on, hypnotized and paralyzed, as money continues to
wreak havoc on the Constitution and the FCC.

I continued by telling the judges, "This seems to
this nonlawyer to be somehow illegal or unethical,
and without a doubt as wrong as wrong can be."

One of the judges stood up and quietly replied,
"Richard, if you had a tough lawyer you could win
that in this court."

We deserve to know exactly why the Fairness Doctrine was gutted and by whom. It is a mistake that
can and should be rectified. It is the source of our
lack of reasoned political debate and knowledge, for
the absence of logic and the tide of senselessness.

We know which Court made the ruling that allows
money to be treated as free speech—a spasm of illogic that spits at the idea of equal participation in
politics, makes a mockery of our radical doctrine
of participatory citizenship, keeps 98 percent of
Americans without financial resources necessary for
a political career, and repeats the reasons we left
the British Empire to begin with: our refusal to be
ruled by a narrow class of the wealthy.

Through this act of senselessness, we have bound
and gagged public discourse. In place of the discussions of issues that would have dominated all the
Sunday news shows in the 1950s and '60s, we see the
press's coverage of the last few presidential campaigns, which look more and more like professional
wrestling than serious investigations of the public's
important concerns. We can't help entertaining the
idea that some questions might not be approved by the
corporate owners of CBS, NBC, ABC, and Fox, because

their own corporate interests in certain issues keep those questions from being aired on their networks, when advertising dictates the length and depth of the news coverage that should be keeping the citizenry really informed.

Which leads to an inarguable fact:

Fewer and fewer Americans comprehend any issue printed on the front page of any newspaper in the country (the few that are left): tax fairness, race, the Middle East, climate change, presidential campaign reform. None of these things get presented on television news with sufficient context, with the background history that explains our national interests, or the issue's impact on the nation. I would argue that no one knows enough about any of these things to develop an informed judgment—not the public, and not the office holders who are supposed to represent them.

This represents a total failure on the part of the media, or our educational system, or both.

Chapter 14

A Civics Initiative

In 2004 I starred in a Broadway show and announced my retirement from film acting before movies had a chance to retire me. Flags all over the country were not lowered to half-mast at my announcement. People didn't spy me on the street and burst into tears, begging me to change my mind.

I went to London, where Mel Brooks had invited me to star in the West End premiere of *The Producers*. At first I had told him, "Mel, I don't know how to sing or dance," and Mel answered, "Oh, who cares? You're funny." And so I accepted. Six days before the first preview audience Mel fired me because I didn't know how to sing or dance.

After I was fired from the production, I decided to stay in the UK for a while. I submitted an idea to Oxford University "to research the damage being done to America by the absence of teaching Civics." They

accepted my thesis, and I became a Senior Research
Advisor at St Antony's College, Oxford.

During the first of four years I would spend at
Oxford, I participated in what was supposed to be
a panel discussion on the BBC. As I was criticizing
modern communication technology, literally mid-sen-
tence, they turned on the lights and threw me out.
Told me I didn't know what I was talking about.

I sat outside the room where the panel was held,
feeling more humiliated than I could remember. Though
my comments were not televised, I was sure the BBC
execs would remember the actor who said such silly
things, making it unlikely I would ever get invited
to a BBC event again, broadcast or not. I would be
whispered about like Robert Taylor in *A Yank at
Oxford*. While I was stewing outside the room, I suddenly heard a shuffle of elderly feet, and I looked
up at an ancient man, old enough to have invented
radio. I braced myself for another caustic grenade,
but instead he said, "You're not crazy. Keep talking."
Another voice joined in, "You're not wrong." Its owner
handed me a card that read "Qualcomm." A Yank! "If
you come to San Diego, call me," he added. His invi-
tation is why, when I moved back to the States four
years later, I settled in the not-so-sleepy town of
Encinitas, just north of San Diego.

I confess that was all I needed to reclaim my
self-worth. I wasn't wrong after all, and the BBC was
going to rue the day. In fact, the network brought
me back, and I began a year of constant enjoyment in
the role of the rule breaker, appearing frequently
on the BBC as an American gadfly. The Great Gadfly.

I hadn't admitted to myself that I missed the university experience I had so carelessly given up earlier in life. Now, forty years later in Oxford, I was
so close to the Bodleian Library that I could inhale

its history every day. I did a jig or drank a pint
or whatever I could think of to express my delight.
I had given up my film career, but I could enjoy as
much Great Theater as I wished. I thought it an even
trade. I also made some wonderful friends at the BBC
during my career as American Gadfly. I was in heaven.

I was on campus every day that first year, but
then I met a woman who seriously changed my life,
and I spent a lot of Oxford time courting her. For
the rest of the four years I attended school less
regularly. Just as Oxford was more than I deserved,
so was she, and I knew it. Marrying her was above my
pay grade. Still is. I also participated in two West
End productions while there, listened to fabulous
lectures, and never thought of Hollywood, even for
a second, until we decided to go back to California.

Oddly, no one seemed to have missed me.

I had accomplished, however, what I set out to
do, which was to learn far more about the American
Constitution, the unwritten British Constitution, and
the reason for the Bill of Rights. I met scholars
from Japan and Ireland, debated with scholars from
Cambridge, and managed to appear on political BBC
TV shows with journalists and modestly claim a 50-50
draw. I have to say that English journalists have
been in a bad mood since the king gave up being king
in 1936 to marry an American, which they seemed to
take out on me even when discussing my acting. However, I was bigger than that and didn't fling contempt
as they do. Maybe I would if I could. Having said
that, I have thus extended my bad press in London for
another decade. If I have fingers when this book is
finished, I'll tell you those stories.

I'm not going to detail all the events and feelings that still make those years resemble a chop-
py crossing of the North Atlantic. I had always

felt embarrassed about becoming a "Celebrity with a
Cause," an actor who takes up precious airtime on the
Oscar broadcast to say one or two sentences about
a real catastrophe somewhere. That usually produces
outrage from those on the other side of the issue
or calls from media for the celebrity to shut up and
be satisfied with her unbelievable hot good looks or
extraordinary talent and never opine about politics
or catastrophes again. Even though I always sided
with the celebrity's right to speak, I would cringe
as they started to give their opinion, desperately
hoping they wouldn't stumble and make the audience
feel the celebrity didn't know enough, thus humiliat-
ing all celebrities. So I decided that this particular celebrity would know his stuff.

In 2006, I created The Dreyfuss Civics Initiative, a nonprofit, nonpartisan organization that aims
to revive the teaching of civics in American public
education, giving generations the critical thinking
skills they need to fulfill the vast potential of
American citizenship.

Some fifteen years ago, I had managed to put
together my first Civics Conference at Martha's Vine-
yard, Massachusetts. There were many guests who participated, including Gordon Wood from Brown University, Frank Luntz the GOP pollster, and the admiral
who commanded the San Diego Naval Station. I asked
the admiral a question: "Is there anything you need
that you don't have?"

"Yes," he answered. "I need more people I can rely
on to understand an order and execute it." Then he
interrupted himself and said, "No, no. I need someone
who knows how to write such an order."

The admiral's answer haunted me.

Years later, I attended meetings put together by a
particularly bright woman, who was and is trying to

create an alternative group to the Council on Foreign Relations, CFR, of which I have been a member for twenty-plus years and counting. At the first meeting I attended in New York, we talked with two men from the FBI. Their titles indicated they were the real deal, the officials who kept the FBI from being politicized when a new president named the next head of the FBI. The new head has to go through the confirmation process and explain changes in direction demanded by the new president, but he is a figurehead. The men in front of us in New York were the men who kept the Bureau even-keeled, who functioned above a certain level of constancy and expertise through all regime changes.

During the Q&A, I asked the gentlemen the same question I had asked the admiral some ten years earlier.

"Is there anything you don't have that you need?"

"Yes," came the reply. "We have less brainpower than we should in the analysis of the metadata we collect."

"In other words, you have all the info gathered from agents on the ground and through technology; you just need people who can interpret the information?"

"Yes, that's correct."

"Can I suggest an idea?" I said. "I assume, though I don't know for sure, that you are prohibited from recruiting into the FBI graduates from foreign universities."

They nodded.

"Then why don't you go to your boss, the Congress, and ask for more rigorous education in the public schools, so you have better potential recruits?"

"Oh, we would never do that."

I blinked. "Why not?"

"That would be considered inappropriate."

I stewed on that for a bit while the discussion moved to other areas. Then . . .

"But, may I please ask—" Now the people sitting around me started to whisper, "Richard. Sshh. Don't. They've answered you, don't go on, Richard."

"No," I whispered back angrily. "This is the national security of my country." Indeed, it was post 9/11, and we weren't at all sure of ourselves in that new world.

I turned to the FBI men again: "You know there are few branches of government that have authority over you. The Department of Justice, the president, and, in many ways where it counts, the Congress. Why don't you approach the Congress, in executive session (privately, and restricted to those in Congress with direct authority), and explain the problem, and demand a higher level of rigor within American education?"

"As I said, we would think that to be highly inappropriate," replied the FBI.

A few days later, I wrote to the lady who was the creator of the conference: "I hope you can see the possibility that the agents from the FBI were lying to us, which I don't necessarily disapprove of. Either they have previously identified the problem and are aware of the need to change the 'facts on the ground,' so they are already taking such actions as we may have stumbled on, or if they weren't lying to us, and they did not know the authority that they are accountable to. If so, I am suddenly frightened in a way I can hardly describe. If they don't know who has authority over the FBI, that's not a pothole, but a sinkhole as large as a football field—a hole in their knowledge of our political system which is unexpected, to say the least."

We are already in far more serious trouble than we know. We may be closer to chaos today than I had originally assumed. According to the FBI, and before that the admiral, our educational system is not serving our national needs.

These are real-world issues we should all be discussing.

Chapter 15

Teaching Active Citizenship

Fareed Zakaria, a respected political analyst, wrote a book a few years ago titled *In Defense of a Liberal Education*. He clearly lays out exactly what I think is needed, with one critical difference. Mr. Zakaria placed the whole effort at the university level. This astonished, even angered me.

That Zakaria didn't see the error is more than disturbing. If he thought that the public school years, when brains are developing their fastest, were not for fundamentals, what was public school for? Just keeping kids off the streets so the adults could breathe easier? A liberal education is left to the universities because . . . well, why? Is it because we think our high school students are too stupid? What about those who for whatever reason won't go on to college? If a complete education is only for those who end up in universities, what happens to the power of the common people?

Arne Duncan, Obama's secretary of education and
a man I have great respect for, once invited me to
attend what they called the Obama administration's
"university level rollout of civic instruction." The
presentation tried to convince me that public school
was not the place for such civic lessons, that only
universities were. I listened, then raised my hand
when questions were asked for, and said, "If I am
correct, this program should cause students' respect
and love for the Bill of Rights, Constitution, and
all that comes with it. But if you wait until students graduate from high school, you are guaranteeing failure. Later in the life of students, it will be
harder to appeal to their affections, because during
adolescence teenagers' brains are rebuilt, neuron for
neuron, from innocent acceptance to skepticism and
cynicism. By college they will greet any attempt to
inspire love for their system of governance with a
middle finger. Bet on it."

I never heard of that particular program again,
and I think I would have heard of it had it been
installed. I'm just saying.

Smart people can sometimes make a whopper of an
error. Perhaps Zakaria, Duncan, and Obama had been
adults for too long.

At first, a child's brain is like the child who
hosts it, unable to perform many things it will
eventually do alone, smoothly and more expertly. The
human child needs a longer parent/child relationship
than any other mammal, except perhaps the elephant.
A human child could not be left to himself without
guardians and survive, not before the age of twelve
at the earliest. Compare that with panthers or lions,
who could measure their reliance on their mothers in
a matter of weeks.

Scientists who study brain development, neurologists

and psychologists, know that abstractions such as metaphor are beyond the capability of human brains until the approximate age of the fourth grade. This is known to educators, because it's not until the fourth grade that history begins to be taught. Until then the child's brain is rooted in mythic or emotional responses to information.

If we don't recognize this, we won't be able to teach them. And it is crucial that we as a society begin with the brains of the young, while they are still forming.

In the book *Five Minds for the Future*, author Howard Gardner confirms that the human brain is not developed enough to understand more than basic communication skills or emotions beyond love and affection until it has attained the comprehension level of a fourth grader. So, speaking practically, we should begin a civics education with American mythology that speaks to the metaphorical heart, telling the Glory Tales of heroes and heroines whom the young can admire and love, and who are stand-ins for the nation. In the earliest stages of the human brain's development, love is the only thing strong enough to construct the connections to our national story. A child under the age of ten can accept and lock in Enlightenment values through the Glory Tales of Nathan Hale and George Washington and Frederick Douglass. Share with them the old hymns to patriotism:

> *"Listen, my children, and you shall hear/ Of the midnight ride of Paul Revere . . ."*
> *" . . . Here once the embattled farmers stood, and fired the shot heard round the world."*
> *"I cannot tell a lie. 'Twas I that chopped the cherry tree."*

These myths are intensely valuable, deeply felt
ways of ensuring love of country. When you see the
laughter or tears of the children, you know you are
succeeding. We don't want them seeing the dark under-
side of our national story, not just yet. Let's get
them safely loving their country before we let them
loose on American History. But don't mistake me: we
must eventually have them confront that history—yes
indeed, and as a mature critical engagement with our
Work in Progress. Capture their imagination first
with "Give me liberty or give me death" before they
learn about Patrick Henry's slaves. But then regale
them with the hero tales of Harriet Tubman and Rosa
Parks.

Every school day they should look forward to tales
about America's origins, the people who were here
before the Europeans came and the people who were
patriots, all doing something that required courage,
inspiration, and intelligence. Such stories used to
elevate bravery over cowardice, and being honorable
over being a liar. Sometimes the story broke our
hearts, ending with a hero or heroine being killed
but saving their comrades with their noble sacrifice.
Sometimes the characters in the stories said something so memorable, so noble, that as we left for the
day a lot of us would be thinking or saying quietly
that line from Nathan Hale or Sacagawea, practicing
to be great ourselves.

We didn't know it at the time, but we were fall-
ing in love with America. The more stories we heard,
the deeper we fell. That was the purpose of those
stories, to let us fall in love with our country, and
it worked just about every time. If our teacher was
a great storyteller, and she told us of George Washington being so honest that he earned a punishment
for chopping a cherry tree, or of Honest Abe Lincoln

fighting to free the slaves, or of our own fathers fighting to defeat Hitler, each story made us admire America more. As we grew older and learned many things that weren't as admirable, like slavery or the genocide of the natives, we were kept from hating our country and remained determined to make it live up to its promises.

As part of my Civics Initiative, I proposed a template for the goals of public schools that relies upon the ability to raise up the intellectual agility of our students.

The history of America, begun in fourth grade, traditionally starts with the first settlements of Europeans. I think that's a mistake because it identifies us as Europeans and the center of the story and allows the native people to be considered as outside that story.

I propose that in fourth and fifth grades students learn the physical formation of North America. Start with the first animal life, then the first humans, Siberians and perhaps Polynesians followed by Vikings, and the history of the native tribes and the conflicts between them. We should teach an equal amount about the difference between the Apache and Iroquois as we do the differences between Spain and France. Then, in sixth grade, turn the students loose on World History—from China, India, Russia, Africa to Cyrus and Darius, Athens, Rome, Genghis Khan, and then "Why Europe?" This will give students a foundation of understanding to build upon from grade to grade.

High school is where we should begin to teach certain basic skills in civil governance: reasoning with logic, understanding opposing views through classroom exercises featuring debate, civil dissent, context skills that reinforce our values of political

sense and balance. Such exercises are as important
as geography, chemistry, and languages, and combined,
they widen the territory of history. These subjects
can complement one another in teaching clarity of
thought. And the overriding reality is that we all
will need clarity of thought long before some may
need the Mercator map.

The goal of public education is not to achieve a
4.0 GPA in all classes. What is far more valuable is
intellectual curiosity and courage, grounded in subjects that are varied and practical: civics, economics, biology, literature, world history, and national
history. They should be able to synthesize each subject so that they understand how literature relates
to politics and how history relates to science.

Education is not simply the study of a subject; it
is also the study of human thought and the creation
of ideas. We need to learn the skill sets that hone
the intellect and the skills that aim for the ability
to stay light on one's intellectual feet and learn
what is necessary, when it is necessary. These give
muscle to thought, and there are no areas of human
endeavor where these skills are not absolutely essential. All classes should aim for a constantly sharpened utility of mind. This means clarity of thought
and of expression. It makes opposing views both wel-
come and necessary.

If these skills are the focus of education, the
result of these classes is the ability to practice
critical analysis with honesty, which is the one talent that requires some emotional maturity to be used
correctly and should be attained by everyone by the
eleventh grade.

If we succeed in this, by the last year of high
school our students will have the faculty and training to conduct a word-for-word study of our national

documents from the Declaration of Independence to
the Gettysburg Address, with particular emphasis on
the Constitution—documents that formed and shaped
not just our country but the modern world. Only with
the gift of critical thought and reasoning can we
see to what extent we have kept to the principles of
the Founders or built on them. Otherwise, these documents are merely parchment with written words but no
substance or value.

And they will need such tools that can help them
parse information to become great citizens. How does
an issue come at us and from whom? Is it relevant, for
instance, how much of our information of the world
comes from textbooks, family, or television or social
media? Might it be relevant to know what percentage
of the news media is owned by one individual? Or two
or three? What kind of questions do we want them to
ask, with the risk that at the end of the day they
won't be the same potential Democrats or Republicans
or Independents as their parents? If we give them the
ability to ask questions and seek their own answers,
will our gods still be their gods, as it were?

We live within an American system that requires
the active involvement of the people, or so we are
told. The whole system is built on the revolutionary
idea that political power is meant to be exercised
by any and all citizens. If American children are
not told that the people are the ones who have the
final civic authority in our system of governance,
that they are being prepared for that as students
and must be ready to assume such responsibility as
adults, then . . .

They don't have civic authority.

Our students need to be turned into active citizens
by the end of their public school careers, by their
graduation from high school. Anyone who disparages

this need or doesn't believe the young should be armed with a real knowledge of our system and its ideals, a clarity of thought and expression sufficient for their participation in civil governance, and the mobility (and nobility) of mind required to deal with real life, however it unfolds—**is a *bad* *parent*, a *bad educator*, a *bad politician*, and a *bad citizen*.**

Chapter 16

The Return to Senselessness

The most important part of civics education is to turn students into active citizens.

Certain things that societies need are so self-evident that it seems silly to need to say them. Imagine a country that didn't teach medicine with the intention of creating doctors. It would have to fill the void with something, illness being one of those pesky problems that can't be wished away, especially when it's your child who is sick. That absence would be filled by snake oil salesmen, people who called themselves doctors but lied, or even well-intentioned people who simply lacked the knowledge and expertise of medicine. The result, of course, would be that you couldn't get medical treatment with any depth of expertise or knowledge, and your child would have as good a chance of dying at the hands of frauds as surviving.

Imagine a country that abounded in wealth of almost all sorts, from natural resources to flourishing industries, and that didn't teach its citizens economics, from the basics of creating a family budget to the more complex levels of the buying and selling of stocks, taxes, saving for retirement, insurance, medical costs, how your money could make you money, investments, and the like. Citizens have to recognize the difference between hearing of an impending financial crisis and knowing what to do about it. They need to have access to answers about who represents their interests and who doesn't, and what consequences we would face if one decision was taken over another.

Again, in the absence of knowing what is going on and who could be relied on, how to clarify problems or which actions were illegal or unethical, we would turn to amateurs or con men (like Bernie Madoff). Citizens of such a country would not know of options they could take to protect themselves. They would not be aware of laws and institutions that could explain the difference between criminal and legal acts, or how to hold responsible those who committed such acts. It would become impossible to know the difference between charlatans and experts.

Imagine a country that chose to be governed by its citizens, acting as representatives of the population as a whole, but who were not taught how to govern. That means not being taught the values that the laws were grounded in or how they differ from other nations' values, needs, and interests. It means not understanding our own needs and interests. That void has vast consequences, because governance is not only immediate but creates the building blocks of the future strength and security of the nation, for the time when your children will be responsible for its quality of life.

So, if people are sovereign, isn't it in the interest of our nation to make sure that people be tutored? Alexander the Great was tutored by Aristotle. The Sun King, Louis XIV of France, was tutored by many scholars. If the monarchs and autocrats were tutored because they held the sovereign power in their societies, shouldn't we all tutor ourselves and our children to preserve the sovereignty of the people in a democratic republic?

If we take upon ourselves the ultimate power in this nation, we should learn about all we are responsible for, since we must decide substantive issues whether they are subtle, simple, or complex. It's not just how large or small the army is or should be. It is, among many things, what needs the nation has, what efforts the nation needs to demand of itself, what foreign powers are helped or hindered by a nation's success or failure. Whose interests are served first, the nation's as a whole, or only special interests within the nation? For that matter, who actually comprises "the nation," all citizens or only some?

One sign of the failure of our civics education is that Americans have forgotten that WE are the government, not THEY. There is no THEY. There is us, with different roles at different times. The public is not a noun, it is a verb; it changes shape from issue to issue. It is all of us, and We in some incarnation or other are failing the whole miserably. Should we all be suggesting that "We the People" have become in some real but oddly unreal way "THEY"? Nope.

There are plenty of special interests, usually monied interests, that want you to hate "big government." That our country has a bit more than 326

million people doesn't enter into this public discussion. We also have one of the world's largest
economies, not to mention its largest military. Like
it or not, any country with a population and global
influence that large is going to have a "big government." Those who are at this minute closing this book
thinking they have finally uncovered the "libtard"
who wrote it are themselves victims of a deliberate
failure to teach our basic civic principles.

**We are the government, and those who tell us oth-
erwise don't want us exercising our power as citizens of a republic.**

We are a nation whose governing should be done
by normal citizens, working without special favors,
getting the people's business done, efficiently and
appropriately.

Unfortunately, too many Americans are willing to
give up the power of active citizenship because they
don't want the responsibility; they just want to be
able to blame others. Thus, no one in this society
is accountable any more. The absence of responsibility looms in every corner, if that makes you feel
any better. It's the schools that are failing, not
the media. No, it's the media. No, it's the parents.
No, it's the voters; no, the office holders. No one
resigns under protest or feels the tug between principle and expediency. No one feels the struggle of
duty over ambition or favoritism. Well, the media is
the schools, and the schools are the parents, and the
parents are the voters, and the voters are also the
office holders who we voted in.

So none of us will be to blame when our American
ideals are merely fables?

We can say all we want that "they" are more powerful, that "they" have stolen something, but follow
up on that "they" and you'll find that THEY are WE,

just unwilling to take the responsibility for being US. As much of an ache in the brain as that may feel, it doesn't change the fact of our being We the People. WE ain't nobody else but WE, and the challenge of self-government can only get harder as we fail to teach it, step by step, year after year. Slip up a couple of years and it's hard to catch up; slip up for fifty, and we've got a problem that can't be fixed overnight. Or as the mayor in *Jaws* says, "We've got a panic on our hands on the Fourth of July."

After fighting with England for the principle of ruling ourselves, the principle that WE Americans are the government, how did we attain such stupidity and arrogance to stop knowing who we are, and that WE are in charge? That is the essence of senselessness. It is the return to the way the world always was before our Revolution.

Part of the audience I am aiming at now consists of students, so take what I am saying as a warning and a dangerous perception of your future: You've been cheated and lied to; you've not been educated as you deserve. If you don't use your sovereign power as We the People, you will lose it forever.

Happily, some of them seem to have gotten the message, somehow. When the kids from the Parkland school stood up after a particularly despicable horror and firmly said "Bullshit," I felt a lightening in my heart. I thought of them, then and now, as evidence that what I had come to fear for my country might be wrong.

Then, in 2018, a lawsuit was filed in Rhode Island, brought on behalf of students who sued the state for failing "to instruct them in the values and skills necessary to participate in a democracy, such as voting or serving on a jury." The students alleged that their "inadequate civics education left them

ill-equipped to exercise their constitutional rights."
Now that could have been a tipping point, provided
the profiteers didn't get in the way.

NEWS ALERT! BREAKING NEWS! THIS JUST IN . . .

Federal Judge dismisses Rhode Island students'
lawsuit.

In October 2020, US District Court Judge William
Smith wrote: "This is what it all comes down to: We
may choose to survive as a country by respecting our
Constitution, the laws and norms of political and
civic behavior, and by educating our children on civics, the rule of law, and what it really means to be
an American, and what America means . . . Or, we may
ignore these things at our and their peril."

Then the Judge threw the case out. This is a tragedy, clearly saying, what I'm about to do, I don't
want to do. The judge was warning us and hoping that
someone would pick up the torch and carry this fight.

The children themselves brought this suit before
the court and were opposed by the state of Rhode
Island, its Department of Education, and agencies
of the state. They all should have been on the same
side.

This may have been a lesson in Civics, but not
necessarily the one we want them to learn. We don't
want them believing that the system is rigged against
them. And don't tell me that the students could learn
such things elsewhere.

We know that education is not confined to the
inside of the schoolhouse. And it is not something
that you "do" and then no longer "do" when you become
an adult. It is a lifelong responsibility to yourself,
your community, and your country. We need to ensure
that we retain the right to be called a citizen of
this country, not just by birth, but by sweat and
a commitment to its principles. I suspect there are

members of Congress, and even a former president or two, who would do poorly if tested on their knowledge of the Constitution and all things Civic. But that's what you get when the people have not been educated to take their job as citizens seriously.

If We the People are not responsibly exercising our power, and if politicians as a result have become the most irresponsible group in the nation (or hadn't you noticed that?), then how can we continue to say that We the People have sovereign power? Isn't that a consequence of not being taught how to use that power over half a century?

Chapter 17

Toward a Healthy Democracy

Civics training enables people with opposing views to learn methods of controlled communication, such as civil discourse in debate, clarity of thought and expression, and the agility one needs to put values and issues in context. Civic tools are also of obvious value in creating a civil society in all of its parts. In the absence of a civil society, all you can ultimately see and hear is the loudest bully in the bar. Currently, without examples of civility, Americans tend to treat opposing views as the positions of enemies. Instead of regarding the exchange of opposing views as normal, Americans hate one another.

But, you might ask, if yelling, screaming, and making fun of an opponent's opinions becomes the norm in the single most-potent utility of information dissemination, is it so terrible? Facebook, for example . . . After all, it's more entertaining—that's for damn sure—than

Robert's Rules of Order or Parliamentary Procedure.
Right?

That's what Mark Zuckerberg thinks. His algorithms
are not designed for truly deep learning techniques;
they are designed in opposition to that, and with Mr.
Zuckerberg's eyes wide open. He is betting that he
can outlast any outrage against his business model,
and that we will fold in the face of the intolerable
thought of losing trolling as entertainment, which is
his real offering. I'd like to bet that he's wrong,
and we will have to contain our gut desire to hang
him. That's a real bet. Any takers?

But if more people choose the yellers, profiteers
like the conceiver of Facebook not being fools, they
will reduce the reasonable content that may not be as
popular in favor of the yelling/screaming team that
makes more profit, and reason will be squeezed out of
the market. Eventually there will be no alternatives
because literally no one will remember them. And at
the end of the day—let's all be grown-ups here—the
buck is the more important piece of the puzzle.

As yelling and screaming become the norm, so weak-
ens the central concept of democracy, which is the
shared space of disparate opinion. A healthy democracy depends on people of unlike minds sharing a
political space and the belief that it's okay to have
different opinions. If the only constant in public
examination of the issues at hand is that the guy who
disagrees with you is an idiot, unworthy to finish
his sentence, and deserving only of being demonized
or canceled, isn't that fundamentally antidemocratic?

We must teach civility, and demonstrate it by example for our young citizens to know it exists. We see
too many terrible examples of uncivil discourse in
political debates and on so-called "news" programs.

We watch speakers interrupting their opponents, who raise their voices to overcome the interruptions, until everyone is interrupting and getting louder and louder, and civil discourse is in the dumpster, burning. Meaning is replaced by pure noise. Language without function is a frustrating and fruitless waste of time. We don't analyze issues any more in public without the melodrama of finger pointing, patronizing dismissal, and name-calling.

If that's what dominates cable news and the internet, more people will tune in and click, since we are, after all, Homo sapiens, and human beings who slow down when we pass a car accident because we hope to see something horrible. And that makes us so human.

Maybe it's too late to teach civility to those at the top, so we need to start at the bottom. Civic training must be introduced early, practiced and honed in every subject, every class where teachers who love what they teach use civility in every exchange between themselves and their students. We need to teach it not as poetry, but fact. If you interrupt, if you shout, and if you attack, if you hold those with different opinions in obvious contempt, you cannot hear what they are saying. You cannot evaluate what they are thinking. Nor can anybody else.

Unless we can debate the issues of our time rationally, we cannot solve them. Otherwise, how simple and easy all our issues must be, since we don't analyze or ruminate over them. It must not be so difficult, these matters of climate change or COVID. It must not be so difficult—these matters of keeping the pay of cops, firemen, and teachers above the poverty line. It must not be so difficult, in forming a more perfect union, assuring justice for all, providing a common defense, or promoting the general welfare, or ensuring domestic tranquility for ourselves and our posterity. It must be simple stuff, because we don't educate our youth with any real care or concern.

Gone are patience, thinking things through, the notion that there are consequences to our actions. We no longer adhere to the notion that wrongheaded action is more damaging than taking the time to learn and understand something. These are values that, for the most part, have been lost in all parts of society. Or am I missing something? Our public plague of mutual hatred can only be healed by an effort by people and organizations of good will who cooperate with one another and do the right thing.

So why are you all laughing?

There was a time that "He's a doer" was a compliment in American society. Now the response is usually, "Yes, but he is doing the wrong thing." And fingers start a-pointin' and ridicule starts a-risin' . . . or worse. Same with "He's a thinker." Those people who might think the questions and answers could be more complex, they quail. They sputter into silence, don't they? Not because they're wrong or someone else is right, but the culture just doesn't support the exercise of rational debate anymore. **Gone is respect for opposing views.**

I had, in my opinion, the best teacher in America: Mrs. Palmer, for seventh and eighth grade American history. She was a Republican, which openly informed her classes, not as a hidden agenda but as part of who she was. My parents were Lefties, union people, either Communist or Socialist. Always appreciative of a good political debate. Mrs. Palmer and my mom were participants in an ongoing discussion about America and the world, and mostly through me as the messenger service. I happily carried the water and the messages between them. The subject was, say, the Civil War,

and with Mrs. Palmer's GOP no longer quite the party
of emancipation from slavery as it certainly had been
at its origins, the back-and-forth would go like this:

"Mrs. Palmer says that even though slaves were
not treated as badly as some say today, slavery was a
long sin, and they were right to end it, although the
North ignored all the signals the South was sending
to end the bloodshed."

"Mrs. Palmer, my mom said that if you could show
her when and where the South signaled a willingness
to end slavery before Lee's surrender, she'd buy you
a hat."

"Mom, Mrs. Palmer said that the best pro-business
lawyer in the country was Lincoln."

"Mrs. Palmer, my mom agreed with you!"

I loved Mrs. Palmer's class because her political
opinions and her view of American history were excit-
ingly different for me, 180 degrees in opposition to
those of my parents. Their America sang a very different song from Mrs. Palmer's. And she made no bones
about it; her beliefs were part of her teaching of
history. She made no effort to hide her opinions from
the view of the class, nor should she. Nor should
she.

Given a teacher like that, I sharpened my mind
and learned our history while practicing the tools
of a civil society. I didn't start out a Communist
and move to the center or the right, I started as a
Left-leaning something and became a civically minded
American lib-o-conserv-o something. What I was not
was easier to say: I was not a Confederate, a Jacobin,
a Know-Nothing, a Wilson, a Coolidge, or a Taft. I
was a product of my own delight in history, so I knew
things, little random things, that had weight for me.

Thanks to my lessons in civil discourse, I learned
to make up my own mind about public issues and public

figures when I was still young. I noticed that Ike was sought as a candidate by both Democrats and Republicans; therefore, he could not be too Nixon-like. Not LBJ. Not McGovern. I loved Bobby Kennedy, but that was more like a teenage crush. I really, really liked JFK, though less as history revealed him. I despised his father.

Are there any men or women who can be considered models of honor and integrity in public debate, showing us the way back to sense? I can think of two from opposite ends of our political life: George Will and Bill Moyers. These are two men who remain in my mind as individuals of decency and rationality, however different their politics may be.

Both have earned widespread respect from more than just me. I know neither personally. I admire George Will for standing by his philosophical principles with honor and courage by leaving the present Republican Party, which has abandoned classic conservatism in the Trump era. I hope he reads this book. More, I hope he agrees with it.

I wish the same for Bill Moyers, who represents the best of democratic and liberal values, including decency and civility. Only men like that can save America.

They should be imitated; they are the living embodiment of our finest attributes. They should be referenced in schools as models of civic behavior, because they are heroes of American common sense.

Chapter 18

Common Sense

Thomas Paine published *Common Sense* at the beginning of 1776. His radical attack on monarchy and calls for separation from England preceded the Declaration of Independence by six months, and it was the first American bestseller. During the following winter, when Washington's army was freezing through an unexpectedly brutal winter at Valley Forge, Paine began a series of pamphlets that he called *The American Crisis*.

The first lines caused men and women to stop, in the rain or snow, transfixed by the words:

> *These are the times that try men's souls. The summer soldier and the sunshine patriot will, in this crisis, shrink from the service of their country; but he that stands by it now, deserves the love and thanks of man and woman. Tyranny, like hell, is not easily conquered; yet we have this consolation with us, that the harder the conflict, the more glorious the triumph.*

Paine ignited the colonies, the army, and General George Washington. His words, logic, and clarity were a bomb bursting over the British Empire, from that moment in 1776 into the future of Western civilization. Historians have often described the "pre-Paine/post-Paine" change in the colonial atmosphere. Before his writings, less than a third of the people of all the colonies were willing to be identified in favor of independence, which meant war, which meant death. After *Common Sense* and *The American Crisis* had been read, shared, and argued over, more and more people throughout all the colonies were willing to risk war and death as a sensible choice. Paine knew England would never freely allow independence. The only way for truly clear thinking and a chance to honestly evaluate humanity's moral progress had to be accomplished by war, bloodletting, death, and victory.

The British Empire was arguably stuck in pre-Enlightenment thinking and unable to see the changes coming, while Thomas Paine's perspective foresaw the end of political structures that had lasted for millennia. Paine saw the impossibility of continuing monarchical power, and in simple vocabulary explained how the technology of the eighteenth century would influence rule across vast oceans to prohibit sensible power-sharing. He recognized that the king would always be months behind events in America, creating misunderstandings that could be interpreted as hostile, while the colonies would refuse to be treated as children.

The run-up to the conflict was now sharpened to a fine point of white heat by Thomas Paine and aimed straight at the new world of the future through clearly considered words, logic, and reasoning that inspired passion and outrage and action.

I want to ignite my country just as Paine did.

We need, right now, what Tom Paine saw was needed then, a brace of common sense like a bucket of
ice-cold water. As America's soldiers were freezing
together, looking at their fingers as they slowly
turned frostbitten, they turned Paine's words over
and over in their minds, discussing them with one
another, dotting their *i*'s and crossing their *t*'s with
the reflection and respect the words were due.

There was a wrongness in their world, and though
they wished otherwise, Paine's writings ruthlessly
forced them to see and feel that wrongness and would
not let them ignore it. They read, they followed his
logic; they came to recognize that in the context
of their relationship with Great Britain they had to
act on those words. Paine clearly illuminated that
moment where a choice was starkly presented between
continued humiliation on one hand, and on the other
a struggle for fair treatment with no guarantee of
victory. A decision for action or inaction had come
upon them. The choice for action, terrifying and difficult; the choice for inaction, far easier but fatal.
In that moment they chose to act, committing themselves to war with the words "Present and Accounted
For."

Two hundred and fifty years later the descendants
of those who made that choice for action seem to be
choosing the other alternative, saying, "Present . . .
but not accountable for anything in particular."

We need such a dose of Common Sense now for reasons
even more perilous. Our current America is unbalanced, the essence of the Republic under threat. What
ails us is almost impossible to see if we choose not
to see it, so America has first to open its eyes, feel
the loss as a loss, and harder than anything else
be willing to become the committed citizenry we once
were and have to become again.

In our current society, however, we are working from a specific disadvantage. We have ceased to tell the tale of Tom Paine, what he wrote, and why. Far more than that, we have ceased to describe to our children what our Revolutionary War created other than independence, and there is so much more to tell. We have ceased to explain how different our country was intended to be from all other countries that existed at that time or that had ever existed. We have to tell the tale of how we shaped the new Enlightenment philosophy that made our governance theory unique, and offered to the world a possible exit from Hell.

Some people will say at this point that I am overstating the situation, that I am dramatizing the story with such a phrase as "exit from Hell." But one of the critical truths we have to face up to is that the real history of mankind has been kept from us. Another is that the enormous achievement of the American Constitution has been downplayed. The difference between the world before the Constitution and the world its creation allowed was larger than *anything* that can be imagined today.

Chapter 19

A Call to Action

We now live in a nation filled with paranoia and conspiracy, convinced that all aspects of government are a scam. Remember that you run this place, whether you believe it or not. This nation is yours to save or lose. There are deeply rooted interests that want you to forget that. Let us make that really hard for them. You can change what ails our county. YES, YOU CAN.

You can't do it alone, true, but if you're supported by a visible education and the invisible culture that treats you like mature citizens, we just might be capable of reviving the ideas that made America such an amazing civilization and inspiration for the world.

If you finish this book and do nothing, then this effort was all for naught. If I speak in front of millions of people about this most urgent topic but no one is moved to action, then it was all for naught.

But do one thing, read the preamble of the Constitution:

> *We the People of the United States, in Order to
> form a more perfect Union, establish Justice,
> insure domestic Tranquility, provide for the
> common defense, promote the general Welfare,
> and secure the Blessings of Liberty to ourselves
> and our Posterity, do ordain and establish this
> Constitution for the United States of America.*

Anybody disagree with that? If you disagree, think
about going somewhere else. I mean living somewhere
else. And if you do agree, I want you to email me
that you are in agreement; **civics@dreyfuss.us** is my
email address. For real.

When I get so many emails I can't count, I will
call for a civic strike. And I'm not kidding. The
strike will be coordinated by time zones to the minute, and at twelve noon everyone stops. You don't
call anyone; you don't go anywhere; you don't buy
anything. No social media, no driving, no work, no
nothing! No one does anything for thirty minutes,
not enough to hurt the economy but certainly enough
to get everyone's attention. Those thirty minutes
stand for a demand of an enhanced civic curriculum
starting in elementary school and continuing through
graduation from high school.

I have other ideas too, such as:

Police: One step to reducing acts of apparent rac-
ism, especially on our streets, is to ennoble the
police, retraining them and placing them on par with
Navy SEALs, attaining the same respect with the same
rigor. Anyone whose job includes using weapons should
be more intensively scrutinized than anyone else and

punished for misusing them. Six months of intensive training cannot do it. They should be taught empathy, and the real meaning of "to protect and serve." The police now receive legal privileges well beyond the civilian citizen; they should be answerable with similar rigor and justice. Police unions should not have the power to protect genuinely guilty cops and should share their legal jeopardy.

Lobbyist Limits: No public official can leave office and become a lobbyist. Ever.

Gun Training: Remember that this is intended to please 80 percent of the public. The NRA has long had an efficient gun safety program that teaches owners how to use guns wisely. It's now voluntary. **Make it mandatory**.

I know many hate the NRA. They see the NRA as a right-wing nuthouse, where crazy people think up ways to hide how crazy they are. On the other side, there are those who think that people who hate the NRA are commies who hate America. But what if we make the NRA the heroes? Not to confuse any of you further than necessary, I don't mean Wayne LaPierre or any of the present administration of the NRA. They are all troublemakers, and even Chief Justice Warren Burger would have had them shackled and tried for various offenses from misrepresentation to money scams. I mean returning the NRA to what it used to be, a platform for responsible gun ownership, not just the mouthpiece for the gun manufacturers, who have hidden behind the skirts of the NRA for too long. Name the companies that fund the NRA, then let's insist they eat their fair share of blame for America's murder problem.

Clean up the NRA, then let them decide which guns are allowed at home and how to control children's access to them. All guns whose only function is to

kill people can be held by the NRA in their own
warehouses, which are not open to the government. If
someone wants to use his "people killer," he has to
pass a panel made up of NRA representatives, local
cops, psychologists, and random citizens. Then target
practice is the only use allowed.

I hope reading this book will give you the courage
to help me and press your own ideas.

I've spoken to several presidential librarians,
and discovered that all of them would be enthusiastic
about connecting all of them with visual technology,
creating the possibility of debates and discussions
that could take place in DC or other central locations
but watched from the various presidential libraries across the country. Students, parents, teachers,
tourists, the public in any and all its incarnations
could watch a live event at any presidential library,
discussions with politicians or political scientists,
members of the Supreme Court, or representatives of
organizations focused on a current issue or contro-
versy. All could listen and watch, and learn.

Imagine an America, dotted with power stations
that reenergize our national ideas in the form of
presidential libraries connected to one another
through modern technology, and all pumping shared
ideas and solutions into the whole of the populace.
Imagine discussing together the various topics of
concern to Americans, from historical subjects like
how the Constitution came into existence to contemporary subjects of interest, such as the virus that has
locked us in and the conflicts over health mandates,
the willingness or not to comply, and the conspiracy
theories that result. Such topics are all within the
public sphere and could be hosted by our presidential
libraries in such a manner that all sides are given

a secular blessing, removing the appearance of the satanic from opposing views.

At the end of World War II a new playwright named Arthur Miller wrote three plays that reintroduced America to itself: *All My Sons*, *Death of a Salesman*, and *The Crucible*. America's perception of itself was stamped with Miller's observations, which were illuminating and fascinating.

I want to initiate an American history play competition, starting in the regional theaters of this country. A play is an oddly efficient way to get the civic values taught in schools into the culture, while spewing forth creative ideas at all points.

The play must be about America: the country that is, the America that might have been, the country that was, and the America that might be. The play could be realistic, avant-garde, a musical, ballet, or opera. One play or more would win a MacArthur Fellowship-sized prize. The competition would be open to all: professional playwrights, housewives, cabdrivers, and immigrants. The play would be evaluated by judges who are theatrically and politically various.

Do that for twenty years and imagine how our public understanding of our history and our pride in America could be transformed. This is the job we handed to art eons ago, and theater has been carrying this obligation on its back quite happily. It preceded film as a combination of commerce and art, and it delivers. *Hamilton* took some liberties with the historical record, but look at how successful it was at turning the attention of Americans to our origin story. When we stop treating our history as if all its characters were corpses or statues, we can learn from their bad behavior as well as their good.

When I reached out to some of the eighty-plus
regional theaters across America about this idea, I
succeeded in talking to thirty-four of them, and got
a preliminary YES from thirty-four out of thirty-
four. This thought experiment existed only in my head
at that point. I was spitballing before doing any of
the homework that might give the theater directors
a clear and detailed picture of the cost of such a
thing. I was merely gauging their interest. Still, I
was so encouraged by their enthusiasm for the idea
that I decided I would come back to them with a formal document.

Finally, astonishingly, in putting together the
curriculum for our sharpened skill sets of intellect, we discovered that from the time of the beginning of the era known as the Enlightenment, there
had never been any research facility, any think tank,
any institute of any kind dedicated specifically to
Enlightenment values. That is as astounding as any
factoid floating around our past, because it was only
during a brief sliver of time that those we call our
Founders were educated. That coincidence casts a
very long shadow, because only then were due process
and the inalienable rights allowed to take root and
flourish.

All the more urgent, then, is the offer from the
one name in our history that truly is of unques-
tioned integrity: the family of George Washington.
His brother's descendants have offered to the initiative 12.5 acres in Charles Town, West Virginia, a
perfectly shaped and sized property called the Happy
Retreat, which could be the home of the Washington
Institute for the Study of the Enlightenment (WISE).
It would be two hours from the Capitol, and three
hundred yards from the largest broadband cable on
the eastern seaboard, with room for a library of all

the Enlightenment writers, and their opposing numbers, and rooms for scholars in residence, panels,
debates and discussions, that could among many other
things be part of the greatest field trip in public
school history.

It would be possible to connect with learning
centers everywhere. Different universities—UC, NYU,
George Mason, Harvard—would be well served by partnering with a facility that is directed toward those
who are preparing for a higher education, and who
could then prepare others in the values of citizenship. The United States population is now thirteenth
or fourteenth in its percentage of college graduates worldwide, *which means fewer who are prepared to
think with agility.*

Conclusion

The soldiers had done their part . . . to the last full measure of their devotion. The rest, then and thereafter, would be up to the living. To the living of all subsequent generations, including this one, Gettysburg left an unending responsibility. A nation built on the idea that all men—all men—are of equal worth and equal rights summons every one of its citizens to a life-long commitment to put that idea into practical effect.
—BRUCE CATTON, *GETTYSBURG: THE FINAL FURY*

This may be the conclusion of the book, but it's not the end . . . yet. If we don't stop creating the Passive Citizen and actively restart the purposeful conscious development of the Participating Citizen, America will cease to exist long before the end of this century. There may be a country called the United States of America, but it will not be the country we have been attached to for so long. The values of our Constitution will be a mockery of our reality. **The end game is already upon us.** There will not be an American society, however imperfect, unless we relearn how to be that society.

You have no excuse not to insist on a better, more focused education for your kids or grandkids, whatever their names will be. Margery and Chuck, okay? They will know you didn't do it because the judgment of history will tell them. Those books aren't written yet, but rest assured they will be. Margery and Chuck will be ashamed that you're related to them, even if you're dead. There's no amount of money, no act on your part, no political opinion you hold that will excuse you. Actually, nothing is being asked of you that you couldn't do in any given afternoon, or a few afternoons. It's not hard, and it's not even expensive. Unless you are willing to support a complete revision of the public school system so that it includes everything from Civics to the Arts, unless you pay teachers what they are worth and resist any effort to structure education for profit, then consider that you are a disgrace to your country. That's not a maybe; that's how you will be remembered. And forever despised.

Let it be said right now that those responsible for undermining the American republic by failing to educate its citizens in civic responsibility are guilty first and foremost. They should be assured that one day they will be perceived as criminals, and the institutions they corrupted will be rebuilt, brick by brick—if time hasn't run out. Will it surprise the systems of education, the press, politics, the courts, that I am referring to them? Anyone who enables the present hysteria and confusion is guilty; all who shout (or whisper) that we should allow money to distort our politics, or knowingly deliver untruths, or cast aside due process, are guilty of collusion in incendiary acts.

The coming decades should be filled with outrage and energy, and a promise by Americans to revive America, and not the pallid pretense of America we live with now.

That's simple, isn't it?

There is a path to civic renewal. You all must act for the good of the nation, for our souls, for the nation we won't live to see, for our children and theirs. We can't allow the very real pearl we had in our hands to be indifferently kicked away.

That's why we're here—to assure the youngest that they have us at their backs, and we will not abandon them. Because . . .

If America goes away, what then?

About the Author

Richard Dreyfuss was born in Brooklyn, New York, in 1947. He has been acting in American theater and films for more than fifty years. He appeared on television in shows such as *Bewitched*, *The Big Valley*, and others for over a decade and worked in theater in Los Angeles from 1963. He started doing features in roles of size in the early 1970s with *American Graffiti*, *The Apprenticeship of Duddy Kravitz*, and *Jaws*. He won the Oscar in 1978 for his performance in *The Goodbye Girl* and was nominated again in 1995 for his performance in *Mr. Holland's Opus*.

In his personal life, Dreyfuss has spent a lifetime championing the democratic process and the foundational blocks of our Republican Democracy. In 2008, he founded The Dreyfuss Civics Initiative to encourage, revive, elevate, and enhance the teaching of civics in American schools. The nonprofit organization's programs are meant to promote the advancement

of civic education, civic virtue, and the role citizens can play in the success of our country. Dreyfuss
has made numerous public appearances on this urgent
need for civic education in our school systems. For more
information, please visit thedreyfussinitiative.org.

Acknowledgments

Svetlana Dreyfuss, Kyle Bowe, David Brin, David Black, Stephen Potts, Ron Blackburn, Larissa Thunder, Ted Baer, Harold Holtzer, Mike Medavoy, Akram Elias, Donna Bojarsky, Carl Borack, Tony Lyons and Jay Cassell from Skyhorse, Emily, Ben, Harry, Seth, Asa, Huxley, Kasey, and many, many others.

Thank you all for your love, support, and enormous contributions in helping me finish this book.